A Photographic Guide to

WILD FLOWERS

OF BRITAIN AND EUROPE

Paul Sterry and Bob Press

D1390131

NEW
HOLLAND

First published in the UK in 1995 by
New Holland (Publishers) Ltd
24 Nutford Place, London W1H 6DQ

ISBN 1 85368 299 3 (hbk)
     1 85368 412 0 (pbk)

Editor: Charlotte Fox

Designed and typeset by D & N Publishing, Ramsbury, Wiltshire.

Reproduction by Chroma Graphics, Singapore
Printed and bound in Singapore by Tien Wah Press (Pte) Ltd

Front cover photograph: Creeping Cinquefoil (Paul Sterry)
Back cover photograph: Common Poppy (Paul Sterry)
Title page photograph: Bluebell wood (Paul Sterry)

Photographic Acknowledgements
All the photographs in this book were supplied by Nature Photographers Ltd. Most were taken by Paul Sterry, the exceptions being the following: Brinsley Burbidge 83lr, 114ul; Robin Bush 36ur, 83ur, 127lr; N. A. Callow 67lr; Kevin Carlson 57lr; Bob Chapman 59lr; Andrew Cleave 32ul, 33lr, 42ur, 57ur, 61lr, 64ll, 71lr, 77lr, 93ur, 98ul, 98ll, 111lr, 113lr, 114lr, 115lr, 117lr, 129ur, 130ll; Geoff du Feu 90ll, Jean Hall 77ur, 93lr, 117ur; E. A. Janes 112ll; D. Osborne 125lr, 135ur.
u = upper, l = lower, m = middle, ul = upper left, ur = upper right, ll = lower left, lr = lower right.

Contents

Introduction

Almost everyone who enjoys the countryside has at least a passing interest in wild flowers. Whether walking in the countryside, along the coast or in woodland the immense variety of plants that abound ensures that there is always something new to discover. The study of wild flowers can be endlessly rewarding and it may be followed with little or no special equipment.

This guide is designed to be taken into the field thus enabling living plants to be examined and enjoyed while remaining undisturbed in their natural habitat. In many countries it is illegal to dig up plants and the extinction of many species has been caused by overzealous collectors.

Plants are among the most important elements in the natural world and hold a fascination far beyond that of mere beauty. While all major plant groups are worthy of study, the largest group of all – those which bear flowers – are of particular interest; included in this group are annuals, herbaceous perennials, shrubs and trees. To most of us, however, the term 'wild flowers' implies the smaller plants and bushes, and it is these which are covered in this field guide.

A basic requirement for any study of, or interest in, wild flowers is the ability to put a name to the different kinds encountered. A wide range of European species is covered in this book to help fulfil this requirement, the criteria for their choice including widespread distribution, common occurrence or the distinctive or attractive nature of the flowers. Some, but not all, the flowers in this guide are common throughout Europe. Others may be locally common or have restricted distributions, such as maritime or mountain flowers. All, however, offer a visual celebration of Europe's rich floral heritage.

Plants are constrained by physical boundaries such as oceans and mountain ranges rather than by the political or economic divisions that rule human society. It is not surprising, therefore, that floral distributions span country boundaries. The geographical range covered by this book extends from Britain and the Arctic tundra of Scandinavia in northwest Europe, south-west to the Iberian peninsula and south-west to Turkey and the Caucasian mountains. The Mediterranean forms the southern boundary and the Atlantic that on the west.

The bulk of this book is devoted to the identification of flowers with photographs and species descriptions occupying the core of the text. To assist the study of wild flowers, however, sections on plant structure, identifying wild flowers, plant hunting and outstanding botanical sites in Europe have also been included.

How to use this book

The species in this guide are arranged in an order which is widely accepted by taxonomists and followed by most other books on the flowers of Europe. Closely related plant families are grouped together and so, in general, plants with similar characteristics appear near each other in the book. Occasionally, plants which are superficially similar but not at all related will be found on widely separated pages.

The photographs

Each main entry is illustrated with a photograph. In almost all cases, the plant is shown in flower, since this is the stage at which it is most obvious and when you are most likely to want to identify it. The species covered in this book range in size from tiny annuals to large perennials and shrubs several metres high. For the large plants, it would be impossible always to show both the whole plant and details of the various parts in a single photograph. Every attempt has been made to select photographs which show diagnostic features or which convey the overall character of the plant. All the plants were photographed in their natural habitats.

The species descriptions

The descriptions provide more detailed information about the plant, concentrating on those characters which will help you to identify the plant. The descriptions comprise the following details:

Common name – in all cases, the most widely used vernacular names have been used.

Scientific name – the common name is followed by the scientific name in all cases. The benefit of scientific names is that they remain the same the world over while vernacular names vary from country to country and language to language.

Height – the height is the range of the upper limit which the plant normally attains. However, growth rates and final size vary considerably with factors including the age of the plant, soil type, the degree of exposure; not surprisingly, exceptions frequently occur. For prostrate species which always grow along the ground, length may be substituted for height.

The main description – the descriptions include reference to all aspects that might be useful in the identification of the species in question, namely stems, leaves, inflorescences and flowers, and fruits. Although the photographs concentrate on plants which are in flower, the text frequently contains a description of the fruits too.

Flowering period – like the height, the flowering period is an indication only and should be treated as such. Flowering times within a species may vary widely depending on both local fluctuations in the timing and climate of the seasons from year to year, and on where in Europe a particular individual plant is growing.

Distribution – the European range of each species.

Habitat – some species have special habitat requirements such as maritime shingle, grassland, woodland or a particular soil type.

Corner tabs – these provide an at-a-glance reference relating to the species family groups. See key below.

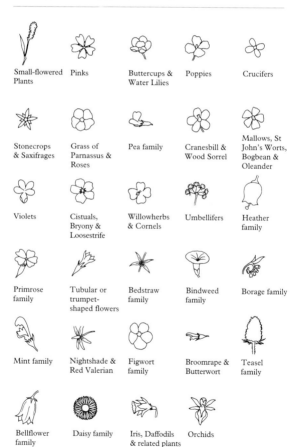

Small-flowered Plants

Pinks

Buttercups & Water Lilies

Poppies

Crucifers

Stonecrops & Saxifrages

Grass of Parnassus & Roses

Pea family

Cranesbill & Wood Sorrel

Mallows, St John's Worts, Bogbean & Oleander

Violets

Cistuals, Bryony & Loosestrife

Willowherbs & Cornels

Umbellifers

Heather family

Primrose family

Tubular or trumpet-shaped flowers

Bedstraw family

Bindweed family

Borage family

Mint family

Nightshade & Red Valerian

Figwort family

Broomrape & Butterwort

Teasel family

Bellflower family

Daisy family

Iris, Daffodils & related plants

Orchids

Glossary

Annual   Taking one year to complete the life cycle.
Anther   Fertile part of a stamen, containing pollen.
Axil   Angle between stem and upper surface of a leaf stalk.
Biennial   Taking two years to complete the life cycle.
Bract   Leaf-like organ beneath a flower or inflorescence.
Bracteole   A small bract.
Bulb   Underground storage organ composed of fleshy, scale-like leaves.
Calyx   All the sepals of a flower.
Carpel   Female organ of a flower consisting of an ovary, style and stigma.
Compound   A leaf having a number of leaflets.
Corm   Underground storage organ formed from a swollen stem base.
Corolla   All the petals of a flower.
Disc floret   Very small, tubular flower with equal lobes.
Epicalyx   Additional whorl or sepal-like segments lying outside the true sepals.
Hemiparasite   Parasitic plant which obtains some of its food from another plant (the host).
Involucral bract   One of the bracts surrounding a head of small flowers or florets; typical of the Daisy family.
Labellum   Lowermost petal of an orchid flower.
Lanceolate   Shaped like the blade of a spear.
Linear   Very narrow, with parallel sides.
Ob-   Prefix applied to shapes, and meaning inverted; thus ob-ovate means egg-shaped, widest above the middle.
Ovate   Egg-shaped, widest below the middle.
Palmate   With lobes or leaflets spreading from a single point.
Parasite   Plant completely lacking green pigment and obtaining all its food from another plant (the host) .
Perennial   Plant that lives for more than two years.
Perianth   All the sepals and petals of a flower.
Pinnate   With two parallel rows of lobes or leaflet.
Ray floret   Very small tubular flower with one side of the apex extended into a long, petal-like strap.
Rhizome   Horizontal, underground stem.
Runner   Slender stem growing along the ground and rooting at intervals to form new plants.
Saprophyte   Plant lacking green pigment and feeding entirely on decaying matter.
Silicula   Pod-like fruit less than three times as long as wide.
Siliqua   A silicula more than three times as long as wide
Spathe   Leaf-like bract, fleshy and brightly coloured.
Stellate   Star-shaped.
Stipule   Leaf-like organ at the base of a leaf-stalk.
Trifoliate   Leaf divided into three leaflets.
Umbel   Umbrella-shaped inflorescence of flowers.

Plant structure

Wild flowers, like all flowering plants, are composed of a variety of different structure, namely stems, leaves, inflorescences and flowers, and fruits. Each one of these will vary from species to species although members of a particular family will usually have characters that conform to a certain basic pattern. It is helpful to understand the way in which these structures are arranged, and the names assigned to the constituent parts, if only to be able to more easily understand the species descriptions in the text.

Stems

These usually robust structures carry the leaves and flowers. In some wild flowers the stems are upright while in others they may be prostrate, the whole plant trailing or growing on the ground. Stems can be branched or unbranched.

Leaves

The leaves are the photosynthetic tissues of the plant, producing food for the plant from sunlight energy, water and carbon dioxide. They are usually carried on stalks and come in a wide variety of shapes and sizes depending on the species concerned. Some leaves are undivided but even in this case, the shape can vary from lanceolate to almost round. Others are divided or indented in a complex manner and reference to the line drawings and glossary should be made.

Inflorescences and flowers

The flower contains the reproductive organs of the plant; some flowers are single-sexed but most contain organs of both sexes. Flowers have evolved to form colourful patterns and shapes not for our eyes but, in the main, for those of pollinating insects. Crowding small flowers together in an inflorescence makes them more visible and attractive to the pollinators.

The overall shape of the flower is largely determined by the petals. It may be radially symmetrical as in Geraniums or bilaterally symmetrical as in Mints and Orchids. Within the flowers, the stamens are the male organs of the flower and consist of a sac-like anther containing the pollen on a slender stalk. The female organs of the flower are the carpels, comprising stigma, style and ovary. The carpels contain ovules which, after fertilisation, from the seeds.

Fruits

The fruits of wild flowers harbour the seeds of the next generation. Their appearance and structure are very varied, ranging from small, single-seeded nutlets to many-seeded berries and large spiny capsules. A simple, practical classification is to divide the fruits into two categories, dry fruits, such as pods and nuts which remain closed, and juicy or fleshy fruits.

Identifying wild flowers

Wild flowers show considerable variation in the structure of the different parts – leaves, flowers and fruits – when the whole range of European species is taken into consideration. At the same time, closely related species may be very similar, differing only in small details; accurate identification then becomes quite a challenge. The diagram below shows the main features of a flower head. When comparing the structures of a plant

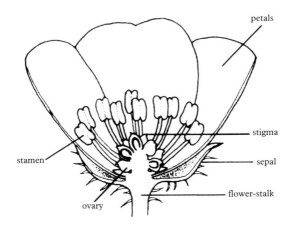

specimen with the descriptions in the text, it is important to be sure you are comparing like with like. Study the section on plant structure in the book before you commit yourself to a decision. Characters which are important for identifying one species may be irrelevant in another and so it is check all the plant's component attributes. The following are among the more important characters to look for.

Habit
This term refers to the growth form of a plant, whether it is erect, ascending, spreading or prostrate. Although this can give a rough idea of the plant's character, it is not fool-proof since a plant may have spreading on even prostrate stems with erect branches and the habit can be affected by environmental conditions.

Stems
Stems offer a number of useful characters, including robustness, colour and degree of hairiness. The shape of the stem in cross-section can be important and whether or not the base of the stem is woody is also significant; the degree of branching can be diagnostic in a few cases.

Leaves

Leaves are very variable and provide a multitude of characters which aid identification. The leaves may be arranged alternately on the stem, in pairs with successive pairs sometimes at ninety degrees to each other, or in whorls. When all the leaves are confined to the base of the stem, they may form a basal rosette.

Leaf size is very variable is only useful in the general sense; the sizes in the text refer to mature leaves on well-grown plants. The overall shape of the leaf, however, can be diagnostic. Shapes vary from very narrow to circular and may be lobed, cut or divided in a variety of ways including pinnate and palmate division.

Flowers and inflorescences

The flowers are often the most visible and obvious parts of a plant; they are certainly the structures that attract the eye and invite closer inspection. Factors such as the number and colour of the petals, their size and shape, should all be taken into consideration when attempting to identify a plant.

The flowers of some plants are solitary but in many species they are carried in complex inflorescences, the term referring to the combination of flowers and any associated structures such as bracts. There are many types of inflorescences, classified by their branching patterns and the sequence in which the flowers develop. These include long, narrow spikes, branched clusters and umbels, which are specialised clusters where the flower stalks arise from the same point. In the Daisy family, the inflorescence, comprising many flowers, in fact resembles a single large flower.

Texture and smell

Although vision is without doubt the most important sense used in plant identification, smell and touch also have roles to play. Fragrances produced by flowers are usually sweet or musky, serving as invitations to pollinating insects. Leaves also can have distinctive smells, especially when rubbed or crushed. While some of these can be pleasant, many are distinctly off-putting and serve as deterrents to herbivores. Leaves have a wide range of textures as well, some being hairy or downy, others smooth and waxy. Use all these clues can be used to help identify the plant in question.

Plant hunting

A major advantage of studying wild flowers is that you seldom have to travel far in order to enjoy your interest. Unkempt gardens and even roadside verges and wasteground have much to offer the botanist, while chalk downs or sea cliffs are a positive delight.

Apart from sharp eyes, the basic equipment needed for observing and identifying wild flowers in the field is remarkably simple. When assembling your equipment for a day out in the field, try to bear in mind the key word 'portable'. It is neither sensible nor practical to take too many items, bulky or otherwise. With this in mind only simple, essential items are described here.

The first piece of equipment is a good quality hand-lens for observing the fine details of the plant. It should have a magnifying power of at least ×10 and you may find the type which incorporates a second lens of ×15 or ×20 very useful.

Serious plant hunters often carry a notebook and pencil to record the details they observe and to make simple sketches. This removes the need to pick flowers or leaves, something which should definitely be avoided.

Nowadays, the popular alternative, or addition, to the notebook is the camera – a very useful means of quickly recording the plant accurately or augmenting your notes. It need not necessarily be particularly sophisticated camera and any number of single lens reflex models are available. It is essential, however, to have some means of taking close-up pictures; a macro lens or extension rings used with an ordinary lens are quite suitable.

One last essential to carry with you is a field guide to help identify or confirm difficult specimens. This guide is designed to be compact enough to fit into a jacket pocket and should enable you to identify many of the more common species you encounter.

Even in northern Europe, wild flowers have something to offer the enthusiast throughout the year. The real botanical interest for this area, however, begins in early spring and extends to early autumn with different habitats being at their best during different seasons. Woodlands offer a riot of ground flora during April and May but wait until June and July before visiting chalk downland or heathland.

Other parts of Europe are, of course, very different from northern Europe. In the Mediterranean, plant growth occurs mainly during the winter months with flowering at its peak from late February to May. In the mountains of southern Europe, however, the growing and flowering seasons are concentrated into a few snow-free months of summer.

Where to go plant hunting in Europe

Some parts of Europe are famous for the floral diversity that they support or for their specialised floras and a brief selection of the major sites for wild flowers is given here. Some are protected at some level to preserve their riches and any specific restrictions or regulations should be checked before visiting them.

Scandinavia
Dovrefjell National Park, Norway. Situated in the mountains of south-central Norway. A largely unforested area of uplands with lime-rich heaths and associated arctic-alpine plants.

North-west Europe
Upper Teesdale National Nature Reserve, England. Situated in the northern Pennines. It comprises calcareous grassland, high moors, hay meadows and cliffs and harbours a rich mixture of northern and southern plants.

The Lizard Peninsula, England. The most south-westerly point of land in Britain with spectacular coastal flowers in May and June.

Fontainbleu Forest, France. Situated just to the south of Paris, the area is a large, state forest with beech, oak and conifers plus many open, sandy and limestone areas. The flora is exceptionally rich and includes many orchids and grassland species.

Duinen van Doorne Nature Reserve, Holland. Situated on the coast of southern Holland. The dune habitats show the full range of succession from wind-blown sand to woodland. More than 700 species of plants have been recorded.

Frankische Schwiz-Veldensteiner Forest Nature Park, Germany. To the north of Nuremburg, this is a partly wooded limestone area with cliffs, caves and calcareous grassland.

The Alps
Hohe Tauern National Park, Austria. A dramatic mountain area in western Austria with pastures, forest and high mountain habitats. The flora contains many alpine species.

Stelvio National Park, Italy and Switzerland. A joint national park that straddles the border near St Moritz. The flora includes lime- and acid-loving plants as well as endemics.

South-west Europe
Pyrenees National Park, France and Ordesa National Park, Spain. Occupying opposite sides of the Pyrenees, these two areas have extremely rich mountain floras.

The Algarve, Portugal. A fantastic area for both Mediterranean and Iberian species. Cape St Vincent is particularly noteworthy with numerous endemic species occurring in the vicinity.

Picos de Europa, Spain. Dramatic mountains in north-central Spain protected by nature reserve and National Park status. There are numerous mountain species.

South-central Europe
Cevennes National Park, France. Situated in southern France this extensive area of limestone and more acid hills harbours a mixture of plants.

Gargano Peninsula, Italy. A large, hilly headland projecting from central Italy into the Adriatic. Habitats include limestone pavement and grassland. Over 2,000 species of plant have been recorded.

South-east Europe
Mount Olympus National Park, Greece. Situated close to the east coast of mainland Greece. A huge mountainous area running down to lowland maquis with mid-altitude woodland. The diverse flora includes many endemics.

13

Common Nettle *Urtica dioica* Up to 150cm

Covered with stinging hairs, this familiar, coarse perennial plant has tough yellow roots and often forms large patches. The four-angled stems have opposite, ovate, pointed and toothed leaves, the lower ones with blades longer than their stalks. The flowers are small, in loose axillary spikes, the males and females on separate plants. There are four greenish petals. The fruit is small, about 1.2mm, ovoid and flattened. Flowers from June to August but the plant can be seen for much of the year. Occurs throughout Europe. Grows in hedges, woods and near buildings. It is usually found on nitrogen-rich soils.

Hop *Humulus lupulus* Up to 600cm

Extensively cultivated for the brewing industry, this perennial climber is bristly with downward-pointing, stiff hairs. The stems are square and twine clockwise. The leaves are opposite, large, ovate and usually three- or five-lobed. Plants are either male or female. The small, stalked male flowers occur in branched clusters. The female flowerhead becomes the hop. Fruit is cone-like and papery. Flowers appear during July and August but the foliage is seen for much longer. Hops grow throughout most of Europe both in natural settings such as hedgerows and woodlands and as cultivated plants for commercial use.

Redshank *Polygonum persicaria* Up to 80cm

This weedy, hairless annual may be found growing erect or sprawling. The stems are often tinged red, as occasionally are the leaves. The leaves are lanceolate and hairless, often with a black spot or smudge in the centre. The basal sheath of the leaf has a long-haired margin. The numerous terminal or axillary flowers occur in densely crowded spikes, each flower being pale pink. Flowers from May to October. Redshank is common in north-western Europe including Britain, with similar species occuring throughout the rest of Europe. It is a weed of cultivated land and waste ground, often with damp soils.

Black Bindweed *Fallopia convolvulus* Up to 100cm

A vigorous, fast-growing, trailing or climbing annual with angular stems that twist clockwise. The leaves are triangular-ovate. The flowers are small, in spike-like inflorescences and greenish-white in colour. There are five petal-like perianth segments, the inner three are narrowly winged in fruit. The fruit itself is 4 to 5mm and dull black. Flowers from July to October. Black-Bindweed occurs throughout Europe including Britain, although it has inadvertently been introduced in the north of its range. It is found on cultivated land and waste ground, usually in areas where the soil has been disturbed.

Sea Beet *Beta vulgaris* subsp. *maritima*   Up to 80cm

A characteristic coastal plant which occurs as an annual, biennial or perennial. It is both sprawling and erect, and often turns yellowish or reddish. The leaves are shiny-green, the lower ones being ovate and heart- or wedge-shaped at the base. The stem leaves are lanceolate. The small flowers are greenish and produced in clusters of one to three, forming a branched spike. Flowers from June to September. Sea Beet grows on the coasts of southern and western Europe, becoming scarce at more northerly latitudes than Britain. Typical habitats include sea cliffs, saltmarshes, shingle and sandy beaches.

Fat Hen *Chenopodium album*   Up to 150cm

A tall and erect annual which is usually covered with a white powdery meal. The stems sometimes have reddish streaks. Leaves are 10 to 80mm long, fresh green in colour. They vary in shape but are usually ovate to lanceolate, often coarsely toothed and lacking lobes. Flowers are produced in an open, leafy spike with long branches. The perianth segments have a raised ridge on the back. Fat Hen flowers from June to October. It occurs throughout Europe and is often very abundant as a weed of waste ground. There are several other, less numerous, related species of waste ground weeds.

Glasswort *Salicornia europea* Up to 40cm

This much-branched, annual plant is characteristic of coastal salt-marshes. The opposite leaves are fused to give the appearance of leafless, fleshy stems made up of short segments. One to three tiny flowers are borne together at the joints of segments. The whole plant usually turns reddish or purple in fruit. A very variable species in terms of height and the degree of branching. Flowers are produced from August to October but the plant itself occurs for a much longer period. It is found around most of coastal Europe and is a locally common salt-marsh plant, usually growing on bare mud.

Common Chickweed *Stellaria media* Up to 90cm

A rather untidy and much branched annual which often overwinters in sheltered spots. The lower leaves are ovate, pointed and long-stalked while the upper ones are more-or-less unstalked. The flowers are prduced in few- or many-flowered inflorescences and are 6 to 10mm in diameter. The sepals are 3 to 6mm long, and slightly longer than the deeply-divided white petals. Flowers can often be found at any time of year although peak flowering is generally July to October. Common Chickweed is a frequent and persistent weed throughout Europe. It is most abundant on disturbed soil and waste ground.

Sea Sandwort *Honkenya peploides*   Up to 25cm

A characteristic plant of the seashore, this creeping perennial has glossy green ovate or oblong, fleshy leaves. Flowers are greenish-white and up to 10mm across. They are produced in axils, or one to six together at the end of the stem. Male and female flowers are on different plants. The sepals equal the petals in male flowers but are longer than the petals in females. Flowers between May and August. Occurs around the coasts of northern and western Europe and is locally common on British coasts. Grows above the high-tide line on both sandy and shingle beaches.

Greater Stitchwort *Stellaria holostea*   Up to 60cm

Usually found rambling among other wayside plants, this perennial has weak, rough and usually sharply four-angled stems. The leaves are lanceolate, pointed and rough on the margins and the underside of the midrib. The striking white flowers are 15 to 30mm across and are produced in loose inflorescences. The petals are cut to half-way and are twice as long as the sepals. Flowers from April to June. It occurs throughout most of Europe although it is rare in Mediterranean regions. Typically found growing in woods, hedgerows and on roadside verges, it is commonest on neutral soils.

Ragged Robin *Lychnis flos-cuculi* Up to 90cm

This distinctive and attractive perennial, has ragged-looking bright pink flowers. The rough stems may be branched or unbranched. The basal leaves are oblong and stalked while the stem leaves are linear-lanceolate and stalkless. The flowers are produced in loose clusters on long stalks, and usually have four-lobed petals. It flowers from May to August and occurs throughout Europe but is rather rare in the south. Damp areas are preferred and it is locally common in water meadows, fens, wet woodland rides and similar habitats. Agricultural drainage has caused a decline in this species in many areas.

Corn-cockle *Agrostemma githago* Up to 100cm

Attractive pink flowers distinguish this tall, hairy annual. Leaves are opposite and linear, their bases joined around the stem. The flowers are solitary and produced on long stalks. The calyx is hairy and forms a tube, and the petals are reddish-purple, notched and shorter than the narrow, calyx teeth. Flowers from May to August. It occurs throughout Europe, but is probably only native in the eastern Mediterranean. A weed of cultivated land, it was formerly locally common in many areas. It has become quite scarce in areas of intensive farming due to the effects of agricultural herbicides.

Bladder Campion *Silene vulgaris*   Up to 60cm

A hairless, greyish perennial, with ascending or erect stems, sometimes woody at the base. The leaves are ovate to linear and often wavy-edged. The flowers are produced in a loose spike, and are often unisexual. The calyx forms and inflated bladder and the large, white petals are deeply divided and do not overlap. Flowers from May to September. It occurs throughout Europe on arable land, waste ground and grassland. WHITE CAMPION (*Silene alba*) has rather similar flowers but with overlapping petals. The calyx is not inflated into a bladder. It grows on disturbed or cultivated ground.

Moss Campion *Silene acaulis*   Up to 20cm across

Moss Campion is one the most attractive and distinctive of Europe's Arctic-Alpine species. A bright green, moss-like perennial, it forms mats or cushions with short, upright stems. Leaves are linear and pointed, and have tough, leathery margins. Individual flowers are 5 to 10mm in diameter, rose-pink and hermaphrodite. Male and female occasionally on separate plants. Flowers are produced in profusion from June to August. Widespread in Arctic Europe and also occurs on higher mountains of western and central Europe at altitudes of up to 2,500 metres. It occasionally grows beside mountain run-off streams at lower altitudes.

Red Campion *Silene dioica* Up to 100cm

A downy perennial, occasionally glandular or hairless. Leaves are ovate or lanceolate-ovate, those on the stem being stalkless. The flowers form a loose inflorescence at the end of the stem and are large, bright pink or occasionally paler, with deeply notched petals. Male and female flowers occur on different plants and appear from March to November. Occasional flowers can be seen, however, at almost any time of year. Occurs throughout most of Europe. In most areas it is common but it is rare in the south. It typically grows in woodlands, hedgerows and along roadside verges, sometimes in great profusion.

Maiden Pink *Dianthus deltoides* Up to 45cm

As its name suggests this tufted grey-green perennial is distinguished by its attractive pink flowers. Leaves are linear-lanceolate and blunt on non-flowering shoots, narrower and pointed on the flowering shoots. Flowers are 12 to 20mm across, and range in colour from almost white to deep pink. These are produced from June to September, and without them the plant is very difficult to locate among grassy vegetation. Found across most of Europe, it is always rather local and especially so in Britain and north-western Europe. Very rare in the Mediterranean area. Usually found in dry, grassy areas.

21

White Water-lily *Nymphaea alba*

Well-known for its round floating leaves up to 40cm across, this aquatic plant can form an almost complete blanket across the surface of ponds and lakes. The lobes of the leaves do not overlap at the base. The top of the leaf is glossy and dark green, while the underside is often reddish. Attractive, floating white flowers are produced from June to September. These are 50 to 200mm in diameter, scented and with up to twenty-five petals. There are numerous stamens and nine to twenty-five yellow stigmas on top of the ovary. White Water-lily can be found throughout most of Europe. It thrives in still, shallow water of ponds and lakes.

Stinking Hellebore *Helleborus foetidus*   28–30cm

As its name suggests, this plant has a particularly unpleasant smell. A sombre green bushy perennial with more or less upright, leafy stems which persist over winter. Leaves are pinnately divided into seven to eleven narrow, toothed lobes from the base. Nodding flowers are bell-shaped and comprise five perianth segments which are green with a purplish edge. Fruits are divided into three pod-like parts, each opening to release several seeds. Flowers from January to April. Occurs in south-western and western Europe as far north as Britain and Germany. It typically grows in woodland and scrub, usually on calcareous soils.

Winter Aconite *Eranthis hyemalis* 5–20cm

A small, early-flowering perennial with basal leaves deeply divided into many lobes. The three stem leaves are similar but smaller, forming a ring near the top of the flowering stem. The solitary stem at the flower tip is 20 to 30cm across and bowl-shaped, usually with six narrowly oval, yellow perianth segments. The fruit usually has six separate pod-like parts. Flowers from February to March. Its natural distribution includes most of southern Europe, from France eastwards to Bulgaria. However, it is widely naturalised elsewhere in Europe and occurs in many parts of Britain and north-western Europe.

Globeflower *Trollius europaeus* Up to 70cm

A hairless perennial, with long-stalked, three- to five-lobed basal leaves, and more-or-less stalkless, divided stem leaves. The globular flowers are up to 50mm across, with ten lemon-yellow, curved perianth segments, the outer ones occasionally being green-tinged. Inside the flower, the stamens and carpels are numerous. Flowers from May to August. It occurs throughout most of Europe although in the south it only grows on mountains. Preferred habitats include damp grassy areas, upland meadows and woods, and on rocky outcrops. Although local, it sometimes grows in profusion in suitable habitats.

Marsh Marigold *Caltha palustris* Up to 60cm

The large, golden, cup-shaped flowers of this creeping, hairless perennial make an attractive sight. The basal leaves are heart-shaped, long-stalked and dark green while the stem leaves are smaller, with shorter stalks. Flowers are produced in a loose inflorescence and are 15 to 30mm across, with five perianth segments. The stamens are numerous and there are five to fifteen carpels. Flowers from March to August, flowering later at more northerly or upland sites. It grows throughout most of Europe but is rare in the Mediterranean. Found in wet places, such as damp meadows or riversides.

Wood Anemone *Anemone nemorosa* Up to 30cm

This hairless perennial is often common enough to form a carpet of delicate flowers on the woodland floor. Flowering stems are upright with a whorl of three leaves two-thirds up the stem. Two large basal leaves appear after the flowers. Leaves usually palmately three-lobed. Flowers are solitary and up to 40mm across. Perianth segments are white, tinged and veined with purple. Flowers from March to May. It occurs throughout most of Europe but is rare in the Mediterranean. It is primarily a woodland flower but also grows in alpine meadows.

24

Pasque-flower *Pulsatilla vulgaris* Up to 12cm

This low, hairy perennial has basal leaves which are silky-hairy when young. Leaves are pinnately divided into feathery segments, and not fully opening until the plant is in flower. Flowering stem has three leaf-like bracts just below the flower. The flowers themselves are 55 to 85mm across and made up of six pale- to dark-purple perianth segments. The stamens are numerous. Flowers from March to May. It occurs locally from western France northwards to Sweden and eastwards to the Ukraine. In Britain, it now occurs in just a few sites in south and east England. Usually grows on old grassland with lime-rich soil.

Traveller's Joy *Clematis vitalba* Up to 30m

This rambling, woody climber with vigorous growth often covers large trees or extensive stretches of hedgerow. It has pinnate leaves, divided into pointed leaflets. The fragrant flowers are about 20mm across, greenish-white or creamy-white in colour and produced in loose clusters. The fruits are feathery and give rise to the plant's other popular name of Old Man's Beard. Flowers from July to September. It is common and widespread throughout southern, western and central Europe although usually restricted to lime-rich soils. Typical habitats include woodland edges and rides, hedgerows and scrub.

Lesser Celandine *Ranunculus ficaria* Up to 30cm

Common enough in many places to form extensive carpets of yellow flowers on the woodland floor. Leaves are heart-shaped at the base with a wavy margin and a superficially variegated appearance. The flowers are 15 to 30mm across and solitary. Each has three sepals and eight to twelve narrow, yellow petals. Flowers have numerous stamens. Flowers from March to May and is usually the first yellow flower to appear en masse. It occurs throughout most of Europe and is common enough in woodlands, hedgerows and damp, open ground.

Meadow Buttercup *Ranunculus acris* Up to 100cm

One of the most familiar summer flowers it is abundant in pastures, sometimes in sufficient profusion to turn fields yellow. A perennial, downy-hairy plant with stiff hairs on the stem. Leaves are deeply divided into three to seven, ovate or wedge-shaped and toothed or further divided segments. Flowers are 15 to 25mm across and comprise five erect sepals, five glossy yellow petals and numerous stamens. They are carried on long stalks. Flowering from May to July. It occurs throughout most of Europe in meadows and damp grassland, sometimes in sufficient profusion to turn fields yellow. BULBOUS BUTTERCUP (*Ranunculus bulbosus*) is similar but has sepals bent backwards and grows on dry, lime-rich soils.

Lesser Spearwort *Ranunculus flammula* Up to 80cm

A relative of the Buttercup but with narrow lobe-less leaves. A rather variable, hairless perennial with erect stems or creeping and rooting at the nodes. Leaves are lanceolate or elliptical, the lower ones being stalked, the upper ones stalkless. The flowers are 7 to 20mm across and yellow, carried on furrowed and slightly hairy stalks and may be solitary or several together. Flowers from June to October. Occurs throughout Europe and is common in suitable habitats in the north-west such as Britain, but rare in the Mediterranean. Grows in wet areas such as marshy meadows and damp ditches.

Pond Water-crowfoot *Ranunculus peltatus* Up to 100cm

An aquatic annual or perennial, usually with both floating and submerged leaves. The broad, rounded floating leaves have three to seven toothed lobes, while the submerged leaves are globose clusters of narrow segments. The flowers are 20mm across and have five white petals. The fruit stalk is usually more than 50mm long. Flowers from June to September. It occurs throughout most of Europe and grows in ponds, ditches and slow-moving rivers. Several closely-related species of Water-crowfoot also occur in the region. COMMON WATER-CROWFOOT (*Ranunculus aquatilis*) is similar but with smaller flowers and divided floating leaves.

27

Common Poppy *Papaver rhoeas* 25–90cm

Easily recognisable erect, branching, hairy annual with leaves divided into toothed segments. The red flowers are 60 to 90mm across, bowl-shaped or flattened, and carried singly at the stem tips. The two green sepals fall off as the flower opens and the four petals often have a dark spot at the base. The flowers bear numerous purplish filaments, each carrying bluish anthers and a disc-like stigma. The fruit is a globose, hairless capsule, opening by pores below a flat top to release many small, bluish-black seeds. Flowers from April to August. It grows on disturbed soils throughout most of Europe.

Yellow Horned-poppy *Glaucium flavum* 30-90cm

A striking plant with large yellow flowers and blue-green foliage. A sparsely hairy biennial or perennial with basal rosettes of pinnately lobed leaves. Branching stems end in solitary, yellow flowers, 60 to 80mm across. The petals are usually uniform in colour but sometimes have a dark spot at the base. The capsule is 150 to 300mm long, slender, curved and hairless. It opens by means of two slits. Flowers from April to September and is locally common in suitable habitats. It is native on the coasts of western and southern Europe and naturalised in central Europe. Grows on maritime sand and shingle, and also on disturbed soil.

Common Fumitory *Fumaria officinalis* Up to 100cm

A rather variable climbing or spreading annual which may be weak or robust in character. Between 20 and 30 flowers are produced in a dense cluster. Individual flowers are 7 to 8mm long, pink with a dark tip. The lower petal has an oval margin while the upper petal is flattened with wings concealing the keel. The sepals are at least a quarter the length of the entire flower. Flowers present from May to October. It grows throughout western, central and southern Europe and is often common in arable fields. The plant may germinate relatively late in the season on newly disturbed soil.

Caper *Capparis spinosa* Up to 150cm long

A deciduous, shrubby perennial with straggly, sometimes spiny stems branching from the base. The leaves are circular to ovate and rather fleshy. The attractive flowers are carried singly in the leaf axils, opening flat, 50 to 70mm across. There are four petals which are white or purplish tinged. The stamens are numerous, long and projecting, the filaments being purplish. The fruit is a rounded berry, about 20mm across; it splits open when ripe to reveal numerous seeds embedded in a sticky mucilage. Flowers from April to September. It is restricted to the Mediterranean region and grows on limestone cliffs and other rocky places.

Wild Cabbage *Brassica oleracea* Up to 300cm

Wild Cabbage is the ancestor of cultivated cabbages. A hairless, branching biennial or perennial with stems becoming woody near the base. The lower leaves are up to 400mm long, with lobed margins and thick texture. The upper leaves are clasping and unlobed. The petals are yellow and 15 to 20mm long. The fruits are 50 to 70mm long, pod-like and carried on spreading stalks. Flowers from May to August and is native on the coasts of Britain, France, Spain and Italy. It invariably grows on maritime cliffs and prefers a limestone bedrock, sometimes occuring near seabird colonies.

Black Mustard *Brassica nigra* Up to 100cm

An erect, branching annual with slender stems. Lower leaves are bristly and pinnately cut, the terminal lobe is much larger than the others. All the leaves are stalked. The small, yellow flowers are carried at the stem tips in small clusters, and the petals are 7 to 9mm long. The fruits are small, slender, beaked and pod-like. They are 10 to 20mm long and pressed against the stems. Flowers from April to September. It occurs almost throughout Europe and grows on any disturbed ground including maritime cliffs and the banks of rivers. It can also be seen along field margins and tracks beside arable land.

Sea-kale *Crambe maritima* 30–75cm

The seeds of this stout and hairless perennial are popular with migrating birds such as finches. Forms clumps of large, leathery, bluish leaves with lobed, wavy or crinkly margins. Its repeatedly branching, ascending stems terminate in a mass of white flowers. Petals are 6 to 10mm long. Fruits are jointed and pod-like, and in two segments: the larger is 7 to 12mm long and contains one seed. Flowers from June to August. It is native on the shores of the Atlantic, Baltic and Black Sea. Sea-kale grows both on maritime shingle and sandy beaches. In suitable habitats it can be quite common.

Garlic Mustard *Alliaria petiolata* Up to 120cm

Also known as Jack-by-the-hedge in many parts of England this erect biennial has distinctive, heart-shaped leaves which are toothed at the margins and smell strongly of garlic when crushed. The flowers are white and carried at the stem tips and their petals are 4 to 6mm long. Fruits are slender, pod-like, ascending and 6 to 20mm long. Flowers from April to July. It occurs throughout most of Europe and is found in open woodland, scrub, hedgerows and roadside verges, especially on lime-rich soils. Leaves are a favourite food of caterpillars of the Orange Tip butterfly.

31

Water-cress *Rorippa nasturtium-aquaticum* 10–60cm

Best known as a salad plant with peppery-tasting leaves that are rich in Vitamin C and iron. A more-or-less hairless perennial with initially creeping, rooting stems which grow upwards to flower. The leaves are dark green, glossy and pinnate, with rounded leaflets. The flowers are small, white and carried at the tips of the stems. The fruits are ascending and pod-like, 13 to 18mm long, with the seeds visible in two rows on each side. Flowers from April to October and is found throughout Europe, except the far north. Grows in shallow, usually running water and is grown commercially for use in cooking.

Cuckooflower *Cardamine pratensis* 30–55cm

Also known as 'Lady's Smock', the plant is perennial with an erect stem and a well-defined basal rosette of leaves. The leaves are pinnate, the basal with one to seven pairs of rounded leaflets. Stem leaves have narrower, more numerous leaflets. Flowers are usually pink but are rather variable and can be purplish or white; the petals are notched and 8 to 13mm long. Fruit is 25 to 40mm long. Flowers from April to July and occurs throughout most of Europe. Preferred habitats include damp grassland and other wet places, usually in the open, and it can be quite common in suitable habitats.

Shepherd's-purse *Capsella bursa-pastoris* 3–40cm

A common weed which grows on waste areas and in gardens. An erect, slender annual or biennial with a basal rosette of pinnately lobed leaves. The upper leaves clasp the stem. The small, white flowers have hairy sepals which are normally green; the petals are 2 to 3mm, twice as long as the sepals. The fruits, from which the plant gains its English name, are heart-shaped, 6 to 9mm long and held erect on spreading stalks. Can be found flowering at almost any time of year, the peak period being from April to October. Occurs throughout Europe on waste areas and disturbed ground.

Wild Mignonette *Reseda lutea* 30–75cm

A bushy, hairless annual or perennial with solid stems and leaves mostly once- or twice-pinnate, the segments of which are linear. The flowers are yellow and small, 6mm across and carried in terminal, spike-like heads. The individual flowers comprise six lobed petals and six sepals. The erect, oblong and warty capsules are 7 to 12mm long. Flowers from April to October. It is native in western and southern Europe and naturalised, but still fairly widespread, further north and east. Grows in grassland and on disturbed, lime-rich ground. In suitable habitats it is common and often forms large, straggly clumps.

Round-leaved Sundew *Drosera rotundifolia* 4–8cm

Capable of digesting insects, this reddish insectivorous perennial has a basal rosette of rounded, long-stalked leaves which are spread flat or only slightly raised. The leaf blades are 5 to 8mm in diameter, and both blade and stalk bear gland-tipped hairs which move to envelope and digest any insect which becomes stuck to them. The flowers are borne on an upright stem and only open fully in bright sunshine. Flowers from June to August. It occurs throughout most of Europe but is absent from most Mediterranean islands and the southern Balkan peninsula. Grows on damp peaty soils in bogs and heaths.

Navelwort *Umbilicus rupestris* 20–50cm

Fleshy, odd, parasol-like leaves distinguish this erect perennial. The blade of the leaf is circular and dished in the centre where the stalk joins, giving rise to the plant's other common name of Wall Pennywort. The leaf margin is shallowly toothed or wavy. Flowers are greenish-white, drooping and carried on a long spike. The individual flowers have a tubular corolla, 8 to 10mm long. Flowers from June to August but the dead flower spikes persist for longer. It occurs in central and western Europe, northwards to Scotland, and grows on old walls, in hedgerows and on rocks, especially acid ones.

Mountain House-leek *Sempervivum montanum* 5–10cm

Popularly cultivated as a rockery plant, this species is resin-scented with sticky leaves. A low perennial, spreading by stolons and with numerous small, crowded rosettes of fleshy, green leaves which sometimes become reddish towards the tips. The leaves are 5 to 10mm long. The petals are usually reddish, but occasionally yellowish, and usually 15 or more in number; the stamens are pale. Flowers from July to September. It is endemic to the Alps, Apennines, Carparthians, Pyrenees and mountains of Corsica. Several other closely related species of house-leek occur in the mountains of Europe; most are also cultivated.

Biting Stonecrop *Sedum acre* 5–12cm

The common name of this evergreen perennial derives from the peppery taste of the leaves. Bright green leaves are thick, fleshy, 3 to 6mm long and elliptical in cross-section. They are crowded and overlapping on the short sterile shoots, but more widely spaced on the longer flowering ones. The flowers are borne in small clusters with spreading branches and are roughly 10mm in diameter. The petals are bright yellow and spreading. Flowers during June and July and it occurs throughout Europe on dry, alkaline soils and sand dunes, and on old walls. In ideal habitats it can form extensive mats.

Rose-root *Rhodiola rosea* 5–35cm

A fleshy mountain perennial with annual stems arising from a scaly crown at the tip of a thick, fragrant rhizome. The bluish-green leaves are alternate on the stem and have toothed margins; the leaf bases often encircle the stem. The flowers have four short, dull yellow petals borne in dense clusters at the tips of the stems. The plants are either male or female. Fruits are orange. Flowers from May to August. It is widespread but rather local in northern Europe and in mountains south to the Pyrenees. Grows on mountain ledges, scree slopes, and sea cliffs.

Meadow Saxifrage *Saxifraga granulata* Up to 50cm

A perennial, dormant in summer, overwintering by means of bulbils. The basal leaves are kidney-shaped, toothed, hairy and often rather fleshy. The stem leaves are few or absent. Small brown bulbils are borne underground in the axils of the basal leaves. The flowers are produced in loose clusters. Petals are 9 to 16mm long and white. It is a rather variable plant which flowers from May to July. It occurs throughout northern, central and western Europe although it is rather local in its distribution. Typically grows in dry, rocky places in the south but in damp grassland elsewhere, including Britain.

Yellow Saxifrage *Saxifraga aizoides* Up to 25cm

This rather loosely tufted, evergreen perennial has ascending flowering stems with much shorter sterile stems. The leaves are fleshy and stalkless, 10 to 25mm long and narrowly oblong; the margins sometimes have small teeth. The attractive flowers are produced in leafy, terminal clusters. The petals are 3 to 6mm long and are yellow to orange in colour, often flecked with red; the petals do not touch. Flowering occurs from June to September. It is widely distributed in Arctic regions as well as in mountains south to the Pyrenees, central Italy and Albania in the east. Yellow Saxifrage grows in damp habitats, often among rocks and stones beside upland rivers and streams.

Purple Saxifrage *Saxifraga oppositifolia* Up to 25cm

Loose mats or compact flat cushions are formed by this evergreen perennial. The thick, opposite leaves are 2 to 6mm long, narrowly obovate to almost circular and dull bluish-green. The flowers are solitary on short, leafy stems. Petals are 5 to 15mm long and pale pink to deep purple; the stamens bluish. Purple Saxifrage is variable in terms of size, petal colour and leaf characters. It is widespread in Arctic Europe as well as mountains to the south. Flowering occurs March to May in most of the region but the later in the year the further north the plant grows.

Opposite-leaved Golden-saxifrage *Chrysosplenium oppositifolium* Up to 20cm

A somewhat hairy perennial with dark bluish-green, stalked leaves in opposite pairs. The margins of the leaves are finely toothed or slightly wavy at the edges and the stalks are no longer than the blade itself. The petal-less flowers are borne in flat terminal clusters with leafy, golden-yellow bracts which are spreading. Flowers from April to June and occurs throughout most of western and central Europe. It is a typical plant of damp, shady habitats such as streamsides drenched in spray, marshy woodland flushes and mountain rocks. In such sites it often spreads to form large patches.

Grass-of-Parnassus *Parnassia palustris* 5–40cm

This beautiful perennial has a basal rosette of leaves and erect stems with a single, stalkless leaf. The basal leaves are long-stalked, ovate to very broadly rounded-triangular, heart-shaped at the base and often red-spotted beneath. The solitary, terminal flowers are 15 to 30cm across and comprise five petals which are white with dark veins. Five stamens alternate with five nectare-bearing structures. Flowers from June to September and grows throughout most of Europe; it is locally common although rare in the south of the region. Damp or wet places such as fens and marshes are the plant's preferred habitats.

Meadowsweet *Filipendula ulmaria* 50–200cm

A tall, striking perennial with leafy stems and non-tuberous roots. The leaves are pinnately divided, the pairs of large, toothed leaflets interspersed with pairs of much small ones. The basal leaves have up to five pairs of large leaflets, each leaflet 20 to 80mm long. The flower inflorescence is up to 25cm long. The numerous creamy flowers comprise five, rarely six, petals, each 2 to 5mm long. The tiny dry fruits are spirally twisted. Flowers from June to September and is locally common throughout most of Europe except for the Mediterranean region. It grows in damp places such as meadows and marshes.

Bramble *Rubus fruticosus* Up to 100cm

This familiar plant is generally considered as a group of closely-related, almost indistinguishable non-outbreeding species. Here, they are treated as a single aggregate which is biennial, with stems that are usually sharply angled and prickly, often arching and rooting at the tips. Leaves of non-flowering stems are usually palmate, with five, toothed leaflets. Flowers are borne in branched inflorescences and comprise white or pale pink petals. The ripe fruit - the well-known blackberry - is black and shiny, with many small segments. Flowers from May to September. Common throughout Europe in most habitats.

Burnet Rose *Rosa pimpinellifolia* Up to 100cm

Most common near the sea, this deciduous shrub with erect stems often forms large, dense patches. Stems are armed with numerous dense, straight prickles and with sharp, bristly hairs. Pinnate leaves have 5 to 11 broad leaflets, each 5 to 15mm long. Flowers are solitary and comprise petals that are 10 to 20mm long, white or rarely pink, and sepals that are erect and entire. The fruit is small, globose and black. Flowers from May to July and occurs throughout most of Europe except the north-east, far south-west and the Mediterranean islands. Preferred habitats include dunes, chalk grassland and limestone areas.

Dog-rose *Rosa canina* Up to 500cm

The arched or erect stems of this deciduous shrub are covered with stout, hooked prickles. The leaves are pinnate and have five to seven leaflets. The flowers are often solitary but are sometimes produced in groups. Petals are 15 to 25mm long and pink or white. The loosely arranged styles are hairy or naked. The fruits are the familiar roseships and are 10 to 20mm long, globose, ovoid or ellipsoid and bright red. Flowers during June and July with rose-hips ripening in the early autumn. It grows in hedgerows, scrub and woods throughout Europe except the far north.

Mountain Avens *Dryas octopetala* Up to 50cm

Often cultivated for garden rockeries this evergreen dwarf shrub has branched, low-spreading stems. The leaves are oblong to ovate with rounded teeth or shallow lobes, and are densely white-hairy beneath. The showy flowers are solitary with eight, white petals, each 7 to 17mm long; there are 7 to 10 sepals and numerous stamens. The flowers face the sun and follow its course during the day. The dry fruits each have a hairy style, 20 to 30mm long. Flowers in June and July. It is an Arctic and mountain species, extending southwards to a line from northern Spain to southern Bulgaria and in suitable areas it carpets whole hillsides.

Wood Avens *Geum urbanum* 20-60cm

Also known as Herb Bennet, the plant is a delicate, hairy perennial. The basal leaves have one to five pairs of leaflets, the terminal one 20 to 100mm long, almost circular and deeply lobed. Stem leaves are deeply three- to five-lobed. Flowers are held erect at first but droop after pollination. The five, spreading yellow petals are 4 to 7mm long. Fruits are hairy, with about 70 in each spherical head. The hairs cling to the fur of animals. Flowers from June to August and grows in shady woods and hedgerows which provide shade. Grows throughout most of Europe and is generally quite common in suitable habitats.

Silverweed *Potentilla anserina* Up to 80cm

A silvery, silky-haired perennial with a rosette of pinnate leaves. The leaves comprise seven to 25 leaflets, each 10 to 40mm long, oblong to ovate and sharply toothed. The flowers are solitary and carried in the leaf axils. There are five yellow petals which are 7 to 10mm long, roughly twice the length of the sepals. Flowering occurs from June to August and Silverweed grows in northern and central Europe, being absent from much of the south. Preferred habitats include bare areas such as paths, roadsides and dunes, often where the soil is damp.

Creeping Cinquefoil *Potentilla reptans* 30–100cm

This creeping perennial has a rosette of persistent leaves and sprawling flowering stems which root at the nodes. The deep green leaves are carried on long stalks and have five to seven obovate, toothed leaflets which are 5 to 70mm long, spreading like the fingers of a hand. The solitary, axillary flowers have five yellow petals, 8 to 12mm long and twice the length of the sepals. Flowers from June to September. Common throughout most of Europe except for the far north and grows in grassy places, roadside verges and on wasteground. In ideal habitats, it can form large and extremely colourful patches.

Wild Strawberry *Fragaria vesca* 5–30cm

Well-known for its delicious fruit, this perennial plant has basal leaf rosettes and long stolons rooting at intervals and producing new plants. Leaves are trifoliate and have ovate to obovate, coarsely-toothed leaflets which are 10 to 60mm long. An erect stem carries a loose cluster of white flowers, each about 15mm across. The bright red 'fruit' is a miniature version of the garden strawberry and is in fact the swollen and fleshy base of the flower; the true fruits are small pips on its surface. Flowers from April to July. It grows throughout most of Europe being found along woodland rides and hedgerows.

Alpine Lady's-mantle *Alchemilla alpina* 10–20cm

A familiar plant to hill-walkers in north-western Europe, this plant is a yellowish-green perennial with ascending stems which are a little longer than the leaves. These are palmately divided into five to seven narrow leaflets that are silvery-silky beneath. The branched inflorescence is composed of many dense clusters of green or yellowish flowers. Individual flowers are small, only 3mm long, with an epicalyx and sepals but no petals. Flowers from June to August. It is found in northern and western Europe, and parts of central Europe, but invariably in the mountains and on acid rocks.

Parsley-piert *Aphanes arvensis* Usually up to 10cm across

Easily overlooked due to its prostrate habit, Parsley-piert is an annual plant with deeply lobed leaves and minute flowers. It may be yellowish- or greyish-green and is much-branched. Leaves are 2 to 10mm long and are divided into three segments, each with three to five oblong lobes at the tip. The leafy, lobed stiplules are joined in pairs about the stem. Flowers are less than 2mm long and borne in dense clusters half enclosed in the cup formed by the stiplules. Flowers from April to October and is found throughout almost the whole of Europe growing mainly on disturbed ground.

Broom *Cytisus scoparius* Up to 200cm

A much-branched shrub with long, straight, green twigs which are five-angled and hairless. In most plants, these stems are erect but in the coastal subspecies, they are prostrate and covered with silky hairs. Leaves are simple or tri-foliate and have leaflets 6 to 20mm long. Yellow flowers are about 20mm long and are borne on young twigs singly or in pairs. Fruits are flattened, oblong pods which are 25 to 40mm long, hairy at the margins and become black when ripe. Flowers from April to June and occurs throughout most of Europe growing in open woodland, heathland and coastal cliffs.

Common Gorse *Ulex europaeus* 60–200cm

This densely branched shrub has green, hairy and almost leafless twigs which are very spiny and up to 25cm long. The yellow flowers are 15 to 20mm long, coconut-scented and scattered on the younger shoots. The fruits are hairy pods which burst explosively on hot summer days. Common Gorse can usually be found in flower at any time of year but the vast majority of flowers are produced in April and May. It is native to western Europe but is planted or naturalised elsewhere. Typical habitats include heaths and rough grassland on acid soils. Flowering occurs from July to September.

Tufted Vetch *Vicia cracca* 60–200cm

A graceful clambering, usually hairless perennial with pinnately divided leaves ending in branching tendrils that entwine adjacent plants. Leaflets are in six to 15 pairs, linear to oblong-ovate in shape and 5 to 30cm long. Its flowers are arranged on dense, stalked, spike-like clusters, 20 to 100mm long, arising from the leaf axils. Flowers range from purple to deep bluish-violet, even on the same cluster. They are 8 to 12mm long with 10 to 30 in a cluster. Fruits are brown, hairless pods, 1 to 2.5cm long. Flowers from June to August and grows throughout most of Europe in scrub and hedges.

Yellow Vetchling *Lathyrus aphaca* Up to 100cm

This distinctive, clambering, hairless annual has pairs of broadly arrow-shaped, leaf-like stipules which are 6 to 50mm long and waxy in appearance; the true leaves are reduced to tendrils. Flowers are pale yellow, 6 to 18mm long, usually carried singly on slender stems which arise at roughly 45 degrees from the axils and may be up to 50mm long. The fruits are brown, hairless pods 20 to 35mm long. Flowers from May to August. Yellow Vetchling is rather local but occurs throughout western, central and southern Europe. Grows in dry, grassy places and disturbed ground, usually where the soils are chalky or sandy.

Sea Pea *Lathyrus japonicus* ssp *maritimus* Up to 90cm long

Usually found on the coast, this hairless, bluish-green perennial has prostrate stems that are rather angled. Leaves are pinnately divided into two to four pairs of elliptical leaflets 2 to 4cm long. Showy flowers are bright purple in colour and are 14 to 18mm long. They are carried in stalked clusters of five to 12 and their petals become blue with age. Fruits are brown pods which are 30 to 50mm long. Flowers from June to August. Grows on shingle beaches and, less frequently, on sand. Grows in suitable coastal habitats around most of north-west Europe and sometimes forms large patches.

Ribbed Melilot *Melilotus officinalis* 40–250cm

A bushy branching biennial which may be erect, spreading, or both. It has trifoliate leaves and produces attractive, elongated spikes of yellow flowers. Flowers are 4 to 7mm long; the wings and standard petals are equal and longer than the keel. The fruits are obovoid, hairless pods which are 3 to 5mm long. These ripen to a brown colour with the style often falling off. Flowers from June to September. It occurs throughout most of Europe but doubtfully native and probably introduced in the north. The plant grows in scrub and on disturbed or cultivated ground, often on clay or saline soils.

White Clover *Trifolium repens* 5–20cm

Extremely common hairless perennial with prostrate stems which branch and root to form extensive mats. Leaves are trifoliate and borne on ascending stalks; leaflets are ovate with a white mark and darker veins, sometimes also a dark mark. The flowers are borne in globose heads which are carried on long stalks. They are scented and white, sometimes tinged with yellow or pink; the individual flowers are 8 to 13mm long. Flowers from April to October and has a widespread distribution, being found throughout most of Europe. It grows in grassy places such as meadows and roadside verges.

Red Clover *Trifolium pratense* 5–100cm long

Bees use the flowers of this downy perennial as a source of nectar. The leaflets are elliptical, 10 to 30mm long and often with a pale, crescent-shaped mark. Stipules are triangular and bristle-pointed. Flower heads are globose or ovoid, 20 to 40mm long and often seen in pairs. They are stalkless, arising from leaf nodes. Individual flowers are 12 to 15mm long, normally reddish-purple or pink in colour, but rarely cream or white. Flowers between May and October. It is native throughout almost the whole of Europe, growing on moist but well-drained soils where it can be abundant. It is also widely cultivated for forage.

Bird's-foot Trefoil *Lotus corniculatus* 5–35cm

The plant's English name is suggested by the shape of the fruits which are slender pods, 15 to 30mm long and splayed like a bird's foot. A creeping or ascending, hairy or hairless perennial with leaflets lanceolate to nearly orbicular and 4 to 18mm long. Flowers are 10 to 16mm long, yellow or reddish-tinged and carried on stalked heads comprising two to seven flowers. The calyx teeth are erect in bud, the upper two with an obtuse angle between them. Flowers from April to September. Occurs throughout almost the whole of Europe growing in grassy places on a wide range of soil types.

Dragon's-teeth *Tetragonolobus maritimus* 10–40cm long

The leaves and stem of this prostrate perennial superficially resemble Bird's-foot Trefoil. Leaves are trifoliate and have a pair of leaf-like true stipules at the base. The solitary, pale yellow flowers are 25 to 30mm long. Fruits are narrow pods 30 to 60mm long, quadrangular in cross-section and with wings about 1mm wide along the angles. Flowers from May to September. Found mainly in central and southern Europe, it is rare in the Mediterranean region and introduced into Britain where it is established in a number of locations. Grows on grassland on clay or lime-rich soils.

Kidney-vetch *Anthyllis vulneraria* 5–90cm

In suitable habitats this very variable annual, biennial or perennial can cover large areas. Leaves pinnately divided with up to seven pairs of leaflets. The stems terminate in compact heads of numerous flowers, with deeply-cut, green bracts borne closely together. Flowers are usually a rich yellow colour but may occasionally have hues of red, purple, orange, whitish or a combination of these; the calyx is inflated and papery. Flowers from April to September and occurs throughout almost the whole of Europe. Grows on grassy and rocky places, from coastal areas up to 3000m in the mountains, usually on lime-rich soils.

Bird's-foot *Ornithopus perpusillus* Up to 30cm long

The splayed fruit pods which resemble a bird's foot, give rise to the English name of this plant. A prostrate, hairy annual with leaves pinnately divided into seven to 13 pairs of elliptical or oblong leaflets. Yellowish-white or pink flowers are 3 to 5mm long, carried in stalked clusters of three to eight, with pinnate, leaf-like bracts. Fruits are narrow and flattened pods, 10 to 18mm long and constricted between each of the four to nine seeds. Flowers from May to August. It occurs mainly in western and central Europe and is found growing on both bare and grassy places, sometimes forming tangled masses.

● Meadow Crane's-bill *Geranium pratense* Up to 80cm

Stunningly attractive, branched, hairy perennial, with leaves divided into five to seven ovate, deeply cut lobes. The cup-shaped flowers are 30 to 40mm across and occur as several in a compact cluster which droops after flowering. Petals are obovate and blue-violet in colour, usually with a network of pale veins. Flowers from June to September and grows in grassland, usually on chalky soil. Occurs throughout most of Europe but is rare in the Mediterranean and much of the far north. Distribution is somewhat patchy, however, the plant being absent from apparently suitable areas within its range.

Dove's-foot Crane's-bill *Geranium molle* Up to 40cm

Usually grey-green in colour, this downy-hairy annual has branched stems that are prostrate or ascending and covered in long soft white hairs, with small glands. The leaves are hairy and rounded in outline. Leaves are divided into five to seven shallow lobes while the stem leaves are more deeply cut. Flowers are 10mm across, pinkish-purple with deeply-notched, spreading petals that are slightly longer than the sepals. Flowers from April to September. It occurs throughout the whole of Europe, except the far north, and is found growing on bare, grassy places such as meadows and maritime dunes.

Common Stork's-bill *Erodium cicutarium* Up to 100cm

This mainly coastal plant is an annual and is usually stickily hairy. It bears pinnate leaves up to 150mm with deeply divided lobes. Flowers are about 20mm across, usually pink, although whitish or lilac examples are not uncommon; up to twelve together are produced in a cluster with brown, leaf-like bracts at the base. Petals are often unequal in size and are easily dislodged. Flowers from June to September and grows on dry and sandy, grassy areas and disturbed ground, often near the coast. It occurs throughout most of Europe although it has been introduced into many areas and is locally fairly common.

51

Wood Sorrel *Oxalis acetosella* Up to 10cm

Wood Sorrel can form extensive carpets of leaves on the woodland floor although these may not always produce many flowers. A low, creeping downy perennial, with a rosette of trifoliate, shamrock-like leaves; each leaflet is round and notched at the tip and the leaves themselves are long-stalked. The flowers are 8 to 15mm across, solitary and carried on long stalks. The petals are white with lilac-purple veins, but occasionally tinged pale purple or violet. Flowers during April and May and grows throughout most of Europe, although it is rare in the south. It grows in woodlands, especially of oak and beech, and other shaded areas.

Dog's Mercury *Mercurialis perenne* Up to 50cm

Carpeting the floor with dark green, this upright perennial is downy-hairy and unbranched. The ovate-lanceolate leaves are shiny green with toothed margins and are carried on short stalks; they are rather crowded in the upper part of the stems but comparatively sparse lower down. Each plant carries flowers of only one sex. Individual male flowers are 4 to 5mm long and carried on long spikes; those of females are on shorter spikes with fewer flowers. Flowers from March to May and occurs throughout most of Europe except the far north. It grows in woodlands, especially under beech, oak or ash.

Wood Spurge *Euphorbia amygdaloides* Up to 90cm

An upright perennial with a softly-hairy texture which grows in often sizeable clumps. Overwintering stems are produced from underground rhizomes and these, in turn, give rise to flowering stems in the spring. The leaves are broad lanceolate, dark green and slightly downy; on the sterile stems, they taper towards the base while the leaves on the flowering stems end abruptly. The flowers lack petals and the umbels have up to ten rays. Flowers from April to June and is locally common in suitable habitats in many parts of Europe including southern England. It grows in woodlands and scrub.

Sea Spurge *Euphorbia paralias* Up to 70cm

After Marram Grass, this plant is one of the first to become established in the shifting dune sands. A fleshy, grey-green perennial, branched from the base with stiffly upright stems. Stem leaves are fleshy, overlapping and ovate; below the inflorescence, the leaves are diamond-shaped. Flowers lack petals and are small with horned glands on the rim. Flowers from April to August. Its distribution is exclusively coastal, occurring in both southern and western Europe as far north as northern England. It is a typical plant of sandy beaches and dunes, being found more occasionally on shingle.

53

Musk Mallow *Malva moschata* 30–125cm

Bright pink flowers distinguish this erect, hairy-stemmed perennial. Upper leaves palmately five- to seven-lobed, each lobe being itself twice pinnately lobed. Attractive flowers have three epicalyx segments which are sparsely hairy. Petals are bright pink and 20 to 30mm long, twice as long as the sepals. They are carried in loose, terminal groups or one to two in the leaf axils. The circular fruit comprises many segments and is clothed with long, white hairs. Flowers during July and August and occurs throughout most of Europe, although it is naturalised in Scandinavia. Grows mainly in grassy places and sometimes forms sizeable patches.

● Common Mallow *Malva sylvestris* Up to 150cm

The characteristics of this plant vary considerably in almost all respects. An erect or spreading perennial with rounded to kidney-shaped leaves are palmately cut into three to seven, shallow, blunt and toothed lobes. Flowers have three oblong-lanceolate to elliptical segments. The petals are 12 to 30mm long and pink to purple often with darker veins and a beard of short hairs near the base. Flowers from June to September and occurs throughout Europe except for the far north. It grows on verges, grassy places and waste ground, often where the soil is disturbed. Common throughout much of its range.

54

Perforate St John's-wort *Hypericum perforatum* 10–100cm

A delicate perennial with tiny black glands on many parts of the plant including the petal edges and sepals. The stems bear two raised lines along their length. Leaves are opposite and ovate to linear in outline; they are more-or-less stalkless and show numerous large, translucent dots. Yellow flowers are borne in large clusters and the petals and stamens often persist. Fruit is a capsule. Flowers from June to September and occurs across most of Europe. It grows along woodland rides and in grassland. Common throughout much of its range, often forming loose but extensive patches.

Marsh St-John's-wort *Hypericum elodes* 10–30cm

Covered with short, white, cottony hairs this perennial plant is a rather unusual, grey-green colour. The rounded stems are creeping and rooting below but with erect forms above. Opposite leaves are 5 to 30mm long with a rounded to broadly elliptical outline. Sepals and yellow petals are persistant. The sepals have fine red glandular teeth and the whole flower is generally closed except in bright sunshine. Flowers from June to September and occurs from western Europe east to Germany and Italy. The plant is invariably associated with wet habitats, generally where the soils are peaty and acid.

Common Dog-violet *Viola riviniana* Up to 15cm

Beautiful, almost hairless perennial and a typical member of the violet family. Leaves up to 40mm, heart-shaped and blunt-tipped. Stipules are ovate or lanceolate and toothed. Flowers are 10 to 13mm across. The sepals are short and pointed and the petals are unequal and broad, blue-violet in colour, the lower one with a light purple spur 3 to 5mm in length. Flowers from March to May, and occasionally also in the autumn from July to September. Occurs throughout Europe except the south-east and grows in woods and grassland. In suitable habitats, the plant is often common.

Wild Pansy *Viola tricolor* Up to 40cm

A familiar hairless or downy-hairy plant with branched stems. It may be an annual, biennial or perennial depending on habitat. Lower leaves are ovate while the upper leaves are oblong; the stipules are deeply divided. Typical pansy flowers are 10 to 15mm across with sepals equalling or longer than the petals. The petals themselves are unequal and yellow, violet or bi-coloured; they are longer than the sepals and the lower one bears a spur up to 6.5mm long. Flowers from April to November. It occurs throughout most of Europe but only on mountains in the south growing in grassland and cultivated land.

Grey-leaved Cistus *Cistus albidus* Up to 100cm

A spreading or erect evergreen shrub with oblong, stalkless leaves densely covered in hairs producing greyish-white appearance. The leaf margins are smooth and even and the hairs are star-shaped. The attractive flowers are pink, 40 to 50mm in diameter and are carried in terminal inflorescences of one to five. The petals have the texture of slightly crumpled tissue paper and are easily dislodged. Flowers from April to June and occurs from south-western Europe eastwards to Italy. Like other cistuses, the plant is typical of Mediterranean maquis habitat where it is an important component of the scrub layer.

Sage-leaved Cistus *Cistus salvifolius* Up to 100cm

As its name suggests, the leaves of this spreading shrub are superficially sage-like in appearance with a wrinkled texture. Leaves are ovate or elliptical in outline, shortly stalked, rough above and rounded or wedge-shaped at the base; carried in opposite pairs on the stems. Flowers are 30 to 50mm across, carried on stalks and produced in loose groups of one to four. Petals are white with a crumpled appearance, the flower has an orange centre and there are five sepals. Flowers from April to June and grows in dry, sunny places around the Mediterranean. Its range includes most of southern Europe.

Common Rock-rose *Helianthemum nummularium* Up to 50cm

Branched wiry stems are a feature of this prostrate or ascending evergreen undershrub. Opposite leaves are oblong, ovate or round in shape, hairless or downy-hairy above, white-felted beneath, and with margins often rolled under. Flowers are carried in a one-sided, one- to twelve-flowered inflorescence. The petals are 6 to 18mm across, usually bright yellow but rarely paler or white, orange or pink, and are easily dislodged; the outer two sepals are smaller than the inner three. Flowers from May to September and occurs throughout most of Europe except the far north. Grows in grassland and on rocks.

White Bryony *Bryonia dioica* Up to 400cm

The fruit of this far-scrambling perennial is poisonous and can be fatal. Plant sprawls vertically as well as horizontally. Leaves are deeply divided into five lobes, approximately the same length. Flowers are carried in axillary inflorescences and are 10 to 18mm across and greenish-white with conspicuous darker veins; male and female flowers grow on separate plants. Fruit is a red berry, 6 to 10mm in diameter. Flowers from May to September and grows across southern, south-central and south-western Europe northwards to Britain; it is widely naturalised elsewhere. Grows in hedges and scrubland.

Purple Loosestrife *Lythrum salicaria* Up to 150cm

Well-known for its purple flower spikes, this striking perennial varies in its downy hairiness. Stem is occasionally branched, with four raised lines. Leaves are either opposite or in whorls of three and are ovate to lanceolate, pointed and stalkless. The flowers are 10 to 15mm across and produced in whorls forming a long spike; the petals are reddish-purple and there are 12 stamens. Flowers from June to August and occurs throughout Europe except the far north. The plant grows beside rivers, lakes and ponds and in damp areas generally, sometimes forming extensive swathes along the margins of watercourses.

Common Evening-primrose *Oenothera biennis* Up to 150cm

Large, showy, yellow flowers, fragrant at night, distinguish this upright biennial. Stem leaves alternate, lanceolate, with finely toothed margins. Flowers 45 to 60mm across comprising four sepals which are reddish and bent back when in flower, four petals, eight stamens in two whorls of four, and a four-lobed stigma. Flowers from June to September. It is a North American plant which has become widely naturalised in Europe, except for the far north and parts of the south. Typically grows on waste ground and disturbed soils and is often seen along railway embankments and motorway verges.

Rosebay Willowherb *Chamerion angustifolium* Up to 250cm

Familiar and showy, patch-forming perennial with long, attractive flower spikes and alternate, lanceolate leaves. Flowers are 20 to 30mm across and pinkish-purple in colour. Structurally, they comprise four petals which are slightly unequal and a four-lobed stigma. The small seeds have a long plume of silky-white hairs which assist in wind dispersal. Flowers from June to August and is widely distributed throughout most of Europe, although it is rare in the south. The plant grows in a range of habitats including cleared woods, heaths, roadsides and waste places; it quickly recolonises burnt land.

Great Willowherb *Epilobium hirsutum* Up to 200cm

Stunning waterside perennial plant, often forming large clumps in suitable habitats. The plant is extremely downy or hairy and the opposite leaves are stalkless, oblong to lanceolate, toothed, with the bases clasping the stem. The impressive flowers are 15 to 25mm across, bright pinkish-purple and produced in groups of one to three together; there are four petals, which are equal and notched at the tip, and a four-lobed stigma. Flowers from June to August and occurs throughout Europe except for the far north. The plant grows in wet areas and is typical of fens and marshes, and alongside river courses.

Dwarf Cornel *Cornus suecica* Up to 25cm

An attractive, creeping perennial herb whose flowers are made distinctive by the presence of showy white bracts, not petals. Stem is upright and the unstalked leaves are rounded or ovate to elliptical and blunt-tipped. The flowers proper are purplish and 2mm across with several clustered tightly together. The clusters are surrounded by four large white bracts which are 30mm across, the whole giving the appearance on a single flower. Fruit is a succulent, red berry. Flowers from June to August. It occurs in northern Europe, including northern England and Scotland, southwards to the Netherlands, growing on moorland, mountains and heaths.

Ivy *Hedera helix* Up to 30m

Well-known, vigorous, evergreen climber or creeper, the stems with clinging, hair-like aerial roots. Leaves are dark glossy green above and paler and matt below; they are three- to five-lobed on the non-flowering shoots and ovate and pointed on the flowering shoots. Greenish flowers, 6 to 10mm across, are produced in a many-flowered umbel. Five petals are at first erect but later bent back. Flowers from September to November and occurs throughout western, central and southern Europe, northwards to Norway. Grows in a variety of habitats typically climbing trees, rocks and walls.

Sea-holly *Eryngium maritimum* Up to 60cm

Despite its appearance this unusual but attractive perennial plant of the seashore is a member of the carrot family. Leaves are bluish-green, leathery and ovate; the basal ones are stalked with very sharp, tough spines and the stems leaves are stalkless but equally spiny. Flowers are small, light blue and produced in a dense, round umbel, 20mm across, with spiny, stalkless bracts underneath; the fruits are densely scaly. Flowers from June to September and occurs all around the coast of Europe, but not in the north. The plant grows on sand or shingle by the sea.

Alexanders *Smyrnium olusatrum* Up to 150cm

Often the first umbellifers to appear in the spring this plant is a hollow-stemmed, hairless and strong-smelling biennial. Leaves are shiny and dark green, divided into three, the terminal segment also being three-lobed. Flowers are yellow, carried on three to eighteen simple umbels in a compound umbel. Fruits are 7 to 8mm across and black. Flowers from April to June, occasionally as early as March in mild regions. It ranges from southern Europe northwards to north-western France and is often naturalised elsewhere. A characteristic plant of roadsides and waste places near the sea but also grows less frequently inland.

Hemlock Water-dropwort *Oenanthe crocata* Up to 150cm

A highly poisonous umbellifer which often kills livestock. The plant is a branched, hairless perennial with hollow, grooved stems, smelling strongly of parsley. The basal leaves are three- to four-pinnate, the lobes broad and wedge-shaped; the stem leaves are two- to three-pinnate, the lobes ovate to linear. Flowers are white and produced in 10 to 40 simple umbels in a terminal compound umbel. Fruits are 4 to 6mm long and cylindrical in shape. Flowers from June to August and is found throughout western Europe. Characteristic plant of wet ditches and damp places such as water meadows.

Fennel *Foeniculum vulgare* Up to 250cm

A familiar kitchen herb with stems that smell strongly of aniseed when crushed. The plant is a greyish-green, hairless perennial with vertically grooved stems. Leaves are three- to four-pinnate, the lobes thread-like and feathery in appearance. Flowers are yellow, carried in 4 to 30 simple umbels in a compound umbel. Fruits are 10mm long, ovoid-oblong and ridged. Flowers from July to September and occurs throughout most of Europe except the north. Probably only native in the south, having been widely cultivated and naturalised for culinary purposes. It is particularly frequent on the coast.

Wild Angelica *Angelica sylvestris* Up to 200cm

A robust and attractive umbellifer which often grows to a considerable height. The plant is a stout and vigorous, upright perennial which is nearly hairless and with a stem usually purple-tinged. Leaves are large and two- to three-pinnate, with oblong-ovate toothed lobes, the leaf stalks forming a sheath. Flowers are white to pinkish; each compound umbel comprises numerous simple umbels. Fruits are 4 to 5mm long, ovoid and winged. Flowers from July to September and occurs throughout most of Europe. It grows in damp places such as woodland rides and meadows, and is often common.

Giant Fennel *Ferula communis* Up to 250cm

One of the largest and most distinctive plants of the Mediterranean. It is an extremely vigorous perennial with three- to four-pinnate leaves, the lobes up to 50mm long and the leaf stalks sheathing the stems. Flowers are yellow and produced in 20 to 40 simple umbels in each compound umbel; flowering heads are more extended than most other umbellifers. Fruits are 15mm long, elliptical in shape and strongly compressed. Flowers from June to August and is found in most parts of the Mediterranean region. It grows on dry ground and is often common on coastal headlands and rocky slopes.

Hogweed *Heracleum sphondylium* Up to 250cm

A robust and roughly hairy or hairless biennial or perennial, with very stout stems. A very common umbellifer, the leaves vary from palmately lobed to pinnate, with up to nine toothed segments; the veins are downy. Flowers are white. The compound umbels, which are up to 200mm across, comprise 15 to 45 simple umbels. Fruits are 5 to 12mm long, elliptical and flattened. The plant contains a blistering agent in its sap. Flowers from April to November and occurs throughout most of Europe except the far north and much of the Mediterranean region. Grows in grassy or rough places.

Wild Carrot *Daucus carota* Up to 150cm

A common, white umbellifer, this plant is a very variable annual or biennial with hairless or roughly hairy stems. Leaves are two- to three-pinnate, the lobes linear or lanceolate, hairy or hairless. Flowers are white, in many small, simple umbels, making a large, flat-topped compound umbel, usually with a single deep purple central flower. There are usually several compound umbels per plant. Fruits are 2 to 4mm, flattened, often with hooked bristles. The compound umbel becomes bowl-shaped in fruit. Flowers from June to September and occurs throughout the whole of Europe. It grows in grassland and is near the sea.

Round-leaved Wintergreen *Pyrola rotundifolia* 5–15cm

A rather low, hairless perennial with a loose basal rosette of broad, rounded leaves with stalks longer than the blades. Flowers are white, 8 to 10mm in diameter; bowl-shaped and spreading and produced in a loose flower spike of five to eight flowers. Prior to opening, the flowers appear globose. Characteristic of this species is the curved style with a disc at the tip. Flowers during June and July and occurs from north-west and central Europe south to Spain, Italy and Bulgaria. It is a local plant, growing in wet places in woods, moors and on sand dunes among wet dune slacks.

Cross-leaved Heath *Erica tetralix* Up to 30cm

An aptly named plant with leaves in whorls of four, members of each pair opposite each other on the stem in a cross shape. A rather straggling evergreen shrub with characteristic pale pink flowers produced in tight, rather one-sided clusters at the ends of upright stems. Individual flowers are inflated and conceal the stamens. Leaves are narrow, needle-like and hairy. Flowers from July to September and occurs from western and northern Europe eastwards to Latvia and Finland. Although a characteristic member of the heathland flora, it is seldom as common as Ling and invariably occurs in wetter places.

Ling *Calluna vulgaris* Up to 150cm

Often referred to simply as 'heather', ling is a small, much-branched evergreen shrub. It has tiny scale-like leaves 2.5 to 3.5mm long, shaped like arrow-heads and pressed against and clasping the stem. Flower spikes are often crowded to form large branched inflorescences. Individual flowers have four pinkish-purple, petal-like sepals 3 to 4mm long and a deeply four-lobed corolla, similar to but shorter than the sepals. Ling flowers from July to September; it occurs across most of Europe but is rare in the Mediterranean region. On drier areas of heathland and moorland, it is often the dominant plant.

Alpenrose *Rhododendron ferrugineum* 50–120cm

An attractive and distinctive alpine plant which derives its name from its deep pink flowers. A twiggy, evergreen shrub, with the young shoots and undersides of leaves covered with rusty-coloured scales. The short-stalked leaves are alternate, 20 to 40mm long and elliptical to oblong. Flowers are about 15mm long and carried in clusters of six to ten. The corolla is funnel-shaped and lobed to about the middle; there are ten stamens. Flowers from May to August and is found in mountain ranges of mainland Europe including the Alps, Pyrenees, and northern Apennines. It grows in mountain woodlands, meadows and rocky places.

Bilberry *Vaccinium myrtillus* Up to 60cm

Also known as Whortle-berries, the fruits of Bilberry are delicious in later summer. The plant is an erect, much-branched deciduous shrub with twigs that are green and three-angled. Toothed leaves are 10 to 30mm long, ovate and bright green with flat margins. Flowers comprise a globose corolla 4 to 6mm across, with short, recurved, green on pink-tinged lobes. The berry is 6 to 10mm across, globose and blue-black with a whitish bloom when ripe. Flowers from April to June and occurs across most of Europe, although only on mountains in the south. Typical habitats include heaths, moors and woods.

Cowberry *Vaccinium vitis-idaea* Up to 30cm

Attractive flowers and conspicuous berries make this a distinctive plant. This small evergreen shrub has a creeping rhizome and erect or arching aerial stems. The elliptical to obovate leaves are untoothed, leathery and dark green above but paler and with inrolled margins beneath. Flowers borne in short, crowded spikes and comprise a white or pinkish, bell-shaped corolla with four or five lobes. The globose red berry is 5 to 10mm across and edible when ripe. Flowers from June to August. Occurs from northern and central Europe south to Italy and Bulgaria. It grows on moors and in woods.

Alpine Snowbell *Soldanella alpina* 5–15cm

A delightful alpine plant, sometimes seen growing through the melting margins of snow patches. A hairless, mat-forming perennial with a basal rosette of long-stalked, leathery evergreen leaves. The leafless stems bear two to four flowers and may double their height in fruit. The nodding, violet or bluish flowers have a funnel-shaped corolla divided to more than halfway, giving a distinctive fringe. Flowers from April to August and occurs in mountains on mainland Europe from the Pyrenees and southern Italy north through the Alps to Germany. It grows above the tree line often on sparse alpine turf.

Primrose *Primula vulgaris* Up to 10cm

A wonderfully familiar spring flower in much of Europe, it is a clump-forming, hairy perennial with loose rosettes of broad, tongue-shaped leaves which are wrinkled, especially towards the margins, and 50 to 250mm long. Flowers are usually pale yellow but may be nearly white in the Balearics, or purple to red in the Balkans. They are 20 to 40mm across and carried singly on long, slender stalks. The fruit is a capsule enclosed within the persistant calyx. Flowers from March to June and occurs throughout most of Europe. It grows, often abundantly, in a variety of habitats including woodland, scrub and hedgerows.

Cowslip *Primula veris* 10–30cm

A delightful spring flower of chalk grassland and other lime-rich areas. A hairy perennial with leaves and leaf rosettes similar to those of Primrose. Bright yellow flowers are funnel-shaped, 8 to 15mm across, with orange spots at the base of each lobe. They are carried in clusters of 10 to 30 on long, naked stalks, the flowers drooping to one side. The ripe capsule is shorter than the calyx, containing dry seeds. Flowers from April to June and occurs throughout most of Europe except the far north and south. Found grrowing in grassland, open woodland and scrub on lime-rich soils, often in large numbers.

Bird's-eye Primrose *Primula farinosa* 3–30cm

This delightful pink-flowered primrose is a short-lived perennial with loose rosettes of shortish, tongue-shaped to elliptical leaves 10 to 100mm long; these are usually densely mealy-white beneath. Flowers are normally lilac-pink with a yellow throat, 8 to 16mm across and carried in a cluster of two to many on a long, naked stalk. Flowers from May to August and occurs mainly in northern and central Europe where it is only locally common; it occurs sparingly in northern England, mainly in Yorkshire. It grows in damp grassland and marshes, usually where the underlying soil is base-rich.

Water Violet *Hottonia palustris* 30–90cm

This attractive and distinctive water plant is an aquatic perennial with both submerged and floating stems bearing leaves 20 to 130mm long and pinnately divided into linear segments. Erect, leafless flowering stems project above the water and carry three to nine whorls of flowers each 20 to 25mm across; these are pale lilac-pink with a yellow throat. The fruits are capsules 3 to 6mm long. Flowers from May to July and occurs mainly in central and western Europe including southern Britain. It grows in shallow, still freshwater such as ditches and ponds, and is threatened by habitat alteration and drainage.

Cyclamen *Cyclamen purpurascens* Up to 15cm

The relatives of this familiar plant whose relatives are often grown as garden or house plants. It is a tuberous and mostly hairless perenial which, unlike other closely related species, produces flowers with the leaves. The leaves are heart-shaped and angled, superficially resembling those of Ivy and sometimes with pale, marbled patterns above and reddish beneath. Flowers are reddish-pink or purplish and are carried singly on slender, reddish, leafless stalks which coil down to the soil-surface as the fruit develops. Flowers from June to October and typically grows on wooded, mountain slopes. The plant's range includes the Alps, Carpathians and Yugoslavia.

71

Yellow Pimpernel *Lysimachia nemorum* 10–45cm

Star-shaped, yellow flowers distinguish this creeping, hairless perennial. This delicate trailing plant has opposite, ovate leaves that are evergreen and 15 to 30mm long. The attractive, yellow flowers are about 12mm across with five spreading petals, carried singly on wiry stalks arising from leaf axils. The fruits are globose capsules about 3mm across. Flowers from May to September and occurs mainly in central and western Europe including most of Britain. It prefers moist and shady habitats and grows in wet woodland, hedgerows and grassy roadside verges. It is widespread but seldom particularly common.

Scarlet Pimpernel *Anagallis arvensis* 6–50cm long

Brilliant red flowers give this well-known plant its name. An almost hairless, prostrate annual with slender, branching stems bearing opposite, ovate to lanceolate leaves 8 to 10mm long. Flowers, which close by early afternoon or in dull weather, are usually red but occasionally blue or various paler shades. They are 10 to 15mm across and are carried singly on wiry stalks arising from the leaf axils; the petals usually have numerous, marginal hairs. Fruits are globose capsules 4 to 6mm across. Flowers from March to October and occurs almost throughout the whole of Europe. It grows on disturbed ground and is often common.

Bog Pimpernel *Anagallis tenella* 5–15cm long

A creeping marshland plant with delicate and attractive pink flowers. A rooting perennial with usually opposite, nearly circular leaves which are 4 to 9mm across and carried on very short stalks. The funnel-shaped flowers are up to 14mm across, and only open fully in bright sunshine. They are solitary and carried on wiry stalks which arise from the leaf axils; the petals are pale pink with reddish veins. Flowers from May to September and occurs mainly in western Europe. It is locally common in fens, bogs and damp, grassy places, generally rambling among low-growing vegetation.

Thrift *Armeria maritima* 5–60cm

One of the most typical coastal flowers, it is a cushion-forming perennial with a branched, woody base producing rosettes of numerous, grass-like leaves up to 150 x 4mm. Slender, erect, leafless stalks terminate in dense, globular flower heads, 10 to 30mm across. These comprise papery calyces and funnel-shaped corollas which are usually pink but sometimes purplish, red or almost white. Flowers at any time between April and October, most in bloom between May and June. Occurs throughout Europe, mainly around the coast but also on mountains up to 3100m. Typical habitats include coastal clifftops and saltmarshes.

73

Common Sea-lavender *Limonium vulgare* 15–70cm

Remeniscent of common lavender but always associated with coastal habitats, this hairless perennial has a woody, branched base bearing sparse rosettes of usually erect, long-stalked, tongue-shaped to spathulate leaves 100 to 150 × 15-40mm. Erect, branching flowering stems bear numerous, spreading spikes which are densely packed with lilac flowers, each 6 to 8mm long. Flowers from July to September and occurs in southern and western Europe including England and Wales. It typically grows on muddy saltmarshes and is locally abundant. The plant is tolerant of occasional immersion in seawater.

Yellow-wort *Blackstonia perfoliata* 10–60cm

An attractive relative of gentians and typical of downland and coastal dunes. This greyishgreen annual has a basal rosette of leaves from which arises an erect stem bearing pairs of ovate to triangular leaves, their bases usually united around the stem. The yellow flowers are carried in a loose, forking, terminal cluster. Each individual flower is 8 to 35mm across with six to twelve spreading petal lobes. Flowers from June to September and occurs in western, central and southern Europe. It is a plant of grassland and bare ground where the underlying soil is calcareous, and of stabilised maritime sands.

Common Centaury *Centaurium erythraea* 10–50cm

A colourful flower of bare, grassy places. A slender, erect biennial with a basal rosette of obovate to elliptical leaves; these are three- to seven-veined and 10 to 50 × 8 to 20mm. The attractive flowers are pink to deep pinkish-purple and 5 to 20mm across. There are five petal lobes and the flowers are carried in loose clusters near the top of the stem. Bright sunshine is needed for the flowers to open fully, and even then they sometimes remain closed. Flowers from April to September and occurs almost throughout the whole of Europe. It grows in grassland and in bare, stony places and scrub.

Marsh Gentian *Gentiana pneumonanthe* 5–40cm

An attractive but declining flower of grassy heaths, this perennial has ascending to erect stems bearing linear to oblong or ovate-lanceolate leaves which are one-veined and 20 to 40mm long. There is no basal rosette of leaves. Trumpet-shaped, blue flowers are 25 to 50mm long, partly greenish on the outside and carried singly at the stem tips and in the axils of the upper leaves. Flowers August to September and occurs sparingly throughout most of Europe including southern England. Grows in bogs and on wet heaths, avoiding lime-rich soils. Locally common in suitable, habitats.

Spring Gentian *Gentiana verna* 2–20cm

A beautiful spring flower of upland and mountain regions. A perennial which forms compact clumps of basal rosettes of broadly ovate leaves which are 5 to 15mm long. Erect stems bear solitary, bright blue flowers which are 15 to 20mm across. The corolla tube is greenish-blue outside with five longitudinal, white lines. Petal lobes are oval and spreading. Flowers from April to June, later at higher altitudes. It has a scattered distribution in Europe, occurring in western Ireland, northern England and in mountainous regions in central and southern Europe. Grows in short grass on lime-rich soils up to 3,000 metres.

Trumpet Gentian *Gentiana acaulis* Up to 10cm

A distinctive mountain perennial which sometimes forms mats. The elliptical or lanceolate leaves are crowded towards the base of the erect stem. The large, solitary, trumpet-shaped flowers are deep-blue and 40 to 70mm long. The corolla has green spots inside the throat and the petal lobes are spreading and pointed. Flowers from May to August and occurs in central Europe and more locally in parts of southern Europe. It grows in mountainous regions, preferring stony and boggy places and usually avoiding lime-rich soils. Several similar species are found on lime-rich mountains in southern Europe.

Bogbean *Menyanthes trifoliata* 12–35cm

A hairless, creeping perennial of wet places, sometimes forming large, floating mats. A distinctive wetland plant, the leaves are trifoliate and held on erect stalks, the obovate leaflets up to 100mm long. Leaves bear a striking resemblance to leaves of broad bean. Star-shaped flowers are about 15mm across and are carried in spike-like heads of 10 to 20; individual flowers comprise five, densely fringed petal lobes which are pink beneath but paler to white above. Flowers from April to July and occurs throughout most of Europe, although it is rare in the Mediterranean region. Grows in wet bogs and fens or other shallow, fresh water.

Oleander *Nerium oleander* Up to 400cm

An attractive shrub which is especially characteristic of the Mediterranean region. This robust and extremely poisonous evergreen shrub has straight, erect, greyish branches bearing linear-lanceolate leaves that are leathery, dark green and 60 to 120mm long. Flowers are usually pink and comprise five spreading petal lobes; the flowers are 30 to 40mm across and are clustered at the stem tips. Fruits are erect, narrow, reddish-brown pods which are 80 to 160mm long. Flowers from April to September and occurs around the Mediterranean region. It grows by water and is widely planted for ornament.

Squinancywort *Asperula cyanchica* 10–50cm

A delightful member of the bedstraw family that grows in grassland. An ascending to erect, tufted perennial with branched, four-angled stems. These bear narrowly lanceolate to linear leaves which are 20 to 35mm long and arranged in whorls of four. The attractive, funnel-shaped flowers are 3 to 4mm across with four petal lobes; pink on the outside, white inside and carried in loose, terminal clusters. Flowers from June to September and occurs locally throughout most of Europe, with northern England lying at the northern limit of its range. It is typically a plant of dry, lime-rich grassland and sand dunes.

Lady's Bedstraw *Galium verum* 50–120cm

The only true bedstraw with bright yellow flowers, although confusion could arise with Crosswort. A sprawling perennial with numerous slightly four-angled stems bearing linear leaves which are 15 to 30mm long; these are arranged in whorls of eight to twelve and have inrolled margins. The bright yellow flowers are 2 to 3mm across and are carried in large numbers in dense but branching, terminal heads. Flowers from June to September and occurs locally throughout most of Europe. It grows in grassland, sand dunes, hedges and in open woodland. The plant is often common in suitable habitats.

Hedge Bedstraw *Galium mollugo* 30–150cm

In most of Europe, this is the commonest, white-flowered bedstraw. It is a sprawling to erect, scrambling perennial with oblong to broadly oblanceolate leaves; these are 10 to 25mm long and arranged in whorls of six to eight. The leaf margins have forward-pointing bristles. The white flowers are 2 to 3mm across and carried in loose, much-branched terminal heads that are ovoid in shape. Flowers from June to September. It occurs throughout most of Europe and is common as far north as the Baltic coast. Typical habitats for this plant include grassy places, scrub, hedgerows and in open woodland.

Crosswort *Cruciata laevipes* 20–60cm

An attractive hedgerow and grassland member of the bedstraw family, this slender, hairy, ascending perennial has broadly lanceolate to ovate leaves; these are yellowish-green, 12 to 20mm long and arranged in whorls of four. The stems are four-angled. The yellow, honey-scented flowers are 2 to 3mm across and are carried in compact clusters in the leaf axils. Flowers from April to June and occurs across central, southern and western Europe including Britain. It grows in grassland, hedgerows, scrub and open woodland, generally preferring lime-rich soils. The plant is locally common in suitable habitats.

Common Dodder *Cuscuta epithymum* Up to 150cm

An intriguing, parasitic plant noticeable by its tangled mass of red stems. A rootless, twining, annual which lacks any chlorophyll and is parasitic on herbaceous plants for its nutrient intake. The red or yellowish, smooth, thread-like stems smother the host plant. Leaves are reduced to scales. Bell-shaped flowers are pink and 3 to 4mm across, carried in globular clusters which are 5 to 10mm across. Flowers from April to October and occurs throughout almost the whole of Europe. It is parasitic mainly on plants of the mint and pea families and is most frequently seen in grassland and on heaths and moors.

Large Bindweed *Calystegia sylvatica* Up to 300cm or more

Like other bindweed species, an extensive rambler that sometimes smothers whole hedgerows. A twining perennial with many slender stems growing from an underground rhizone. Alternate leaves are heart- to arrow-shaped and up to 150mm long. The showy, trumpet-shaped flowers are 60 to 75mm across and are pure white or with five pale pink stripes. Two large, overlapping bracteoles, 14 to 50mm across, completely conceal the calyx. Flowers from July to September. Native to southern Europe but widely naturalised elsewhere, including Britain, near cultivated land and scrub. HEDGE BINDWEED (*Calystegia sepium*) is similar but with 40mm flowers.

Field Bindweed *Convolvulus arvensis* Up to 200cm

A climber with attractive funnel-shaped flowers. A creeping or twining perennial with slender stems branched from the base and growing from pale, fleshy, underground rhizomes. Arrow-shaped leaves are 20 to 50mm long, with backward-pointing or spreading, basal lobes. Flowers are white, pink or longitudinally striped and up to 30mm across, carried in stalked clusters of one to two from the leaf axils. Flowers from June to September and occurs almost throughout the whole of Europe. It typically grows on disturbed ground, roadside verges and coastal grassland, and can be a troublesome weed on cultivation.

●**Viper's-bugloss** *Echium vulgare* 20–90cm

A popular bee plant, this slightly hispid biennial has a basal rosette of leaves and erect flowering stems covered with red-based bristles. The hairy leaves are elliptical to narrowly lanceolate and 50 to 150mm long. Flowers are funnel-shaped and 10 to 19mm long. In bud they are pink but they become blue when open; they are carried in erect spikes or short, downcurved, axillary sprays. Flowers from May to September and occurs almost throughout the whole of Europe except the far north. The plant grows on bare ground and maritime sand and shingle and is very variable in appearance.

Although a hybrid between Common Comfrey and Rough Comprey, the plant is stable and a widespread example of the comfrey family in Europe. An erect, bristly perennial with ovate-lanceolate basal leaves 15 to 250mm long. Leaf bases extend for a short distance down the stems as wings. Tubular, bell-shaped flowers are 13 to 19mm long and are violet, or open pink but then turn blue. Flowers from June to August and is widely naturalised in northern Europe including Britain. Grows along roadsides and beside tracks, and is less dependant on damp soils than other comfrey species.

Borage *Borago officinalis* 15–70mm

Bees and other insects find the flowers of Borage irresistable. The plant is an erect, bristly annual with stalked, ovate to lanceolate basal leaves, 50 to 200mm long, and stalkless, clasping upper leaves. The attractive blue flowers are 20 to 25mm across and carried in loose, arching sprays, the individual flowers facing downwards. The corolla has five, spreading, lanceolate, pointed petal lobes; the stamens and stigma form a central cone. Flowers from April to September and has a natural range that includes most of southern Europe; it is also cultivated and widely naturalised further north. It thrives best on disturbed ground.

Water Forget-me-not *Myosotis scorpioides* Up to 100cm

The commonest forget-me-not species to be found in watery habitats. A perennial with a creeping rhizome and runners. Ascending or erect stems bear oblong to oblong-lanceolate leaves up to 100mm long. The flowers, which are typcial of forget-me-not species, are blue with a central yellow eye and up to 8mm across. Flowers from May to September and is widespread throughout northern and central Europe in suitable habitats. It grows beside fresh water, with the plant often partly submerged; where the underlying soil is neutral or basic, it can be rather common.

Wood Forget-me-not *Myosotis sylvatica* Up to 50cm

A typical forget-me-not species of damp, shady positions. A leafy, much-branched biennial or perennial. It is rather similar in appearance, if not habitat choice, to Water Forget-me-not but lacks this species' runners. The leaves are broadly ovate to elliptical and up to 80mm long. The blue flowers have a central yellow eye; they are usually up to 8mm across but are often markedly smaller. Flowers from April to August and occurs throughout most of Europe where is it generally common everywhere except in the north. It grows along shady woodland rides and in damp, shady grassland.

Hound's-tongue *Cynoglossum officinale* 30–60cm

This plant's unusual name derives from the shape of its leaves. It is an erect, greyish-green, hairy biennial with oblong to lanceolate leaves up to 250mm long. The dull purple, broadly funnel-shaped flowers are up to 10mm across and carried in arching, terminal sprays. The button-like fruits comprise four ovoid nutlets held in the persistent calyx, each with a thickened margin and covered with hooked bristles. Flowers from May to August and occurs across most of Europe except the far north. It grows in dry, grassy places and is particularly common near the coast, often on maritime sands.

Bugle *Ajuga reptans* 10–40cm

A distinctive member of the mint family producing spikes of colourful flowers. A creeping perennial with long, leafy runners and basal rosettes of ovate leaves, 25 to 90mm long. Erect flowering stems are four-angled and hairy on two opposite faces, these alternating between each joint. Blue flowers are 14 to 17mm long and carried in dense spikes with leaf-like bracts often themselves blue-tinged. The corolla has one five-lobed lip. Flowers from April to June and is found throughout most of Europe as far north as southern Scandinavia. It is a characteristic plant of damp woodland rides, scrub and grassland.

Ground Pine *Ajuga chamaepitys* 5–30cm

An aptly-named plant with leaves resembling pine needles which smell of pine when crushed. A usually hairy annual or short-lived perennial. The leaves and bracts are divided into three linear segments 0.5 to 3mm wide, which may be three-lobed at the tips. Flowers are 7 to 25mm long and delicately red- or purple-spotted, two to four at each joint. The corolla has a single five-lobed lip and the flowers are produced rather sparingly. Flowers from May to September and occurs across most of Europe except the north. It grows on stony ground and was formerly a cornfield 'weed'.

Wood Sage *Teucrium scorodonia* 15–50cm

An attractive herb with tall spikes of flowers, often growing in clumps. A hairy perennial with erect, branching stems bearing triangular-ovate, wrinkled leaves which are sage-scented. Pale greenish-yellow flowers are about 9mm long and carried in erect spikes up to 150mm long. In common with other species of *Teucrium*, the corolla has a single five-lobed lip. Flowers from July to September and occurs in southern, western and central Europe as far north as the Baltic coast. Often grows in dry woodland but is also found in scrub, heaths, scree and stable sand dunes, mostly on acid soils.

85

Bastard Balm *Melittis melissophyllum* 20–70cm

One of the most showy members of the mint family, this erect, stong-smelling perennial has hairy stems bearing opposite, oblong to ovate, toothed leaves 20 to 150cm long. White, pink, purple or parti-coloured flowers 25 to 40mm long are carried in whorls of two to six in the axils of leaf-like bracts. The upper lip of the corolla is weakly hooded and the lower lip is three-lobed. Flowers from May to July and occurs in southern, central and western Europe. Fairly common south of its range, rare in southern England. Grows in open woodland, hedgerows and shady, rocky places.

White Dead-nettle *Lamium album* 20–80cm

Superficially similar to common nettle but unrelated, stingless and with attractive, white flowers. A hairy, slightly aromatic perennial with creeping, underground stems and erect, flowering shoots. Opposite leaves are ovate or ovate-oblong, toothed and 25 to 120mm long. White flowers are 20 to 25mm long, with a hooded upper lip. They are carried in rather dense whorls. Flowers from March to December and occurs across most of Europe; throughout most of its range, including Britain, it is common but it is rare in the southern Europe. The plant grows in hedgerows, roadside verges and waste areas.

Yellow Archangel *Lamiastrum galeobdolon* 15–60cm

This colourful, spring hedgerow plant is a hairy perennial. It has long, leafy, creeping runners and erect flowering stems. The opposite leaves are ovate to almost circular, coarsely toothed and 30 to 80mm long. Bright yellow flowers are 14 to 25mm long and carried in whorls around the stem; the upper lip is hooded and the lower lip has brownish markings. Flowers during May and June and occurs across most of Europe including Britain. It can be found growing in woodlands, hedgerows and other shady places and is locally common in much of its range. The plant sometimes grows in fairly extensive stands.

Hedge Woundwort *Stachys sylvatica* 30–120cm

An elegantly flowered herb with a rather unpleasant smell. A hairy, aromatic perennial with erect stems arising from a rhizome. The opposite leaves are heart-shaped, pointed, 40 to 140mm long and with toothed margins. The flowers are dull reddish-purple and carried in whorls which are grouped into spikes. The corollas are 13 to 18mm long with white margins. Flowers from June to October and is found across most of Europe except in the Mediterranean region. Can be found growing in hedgerows and other shady places and is common throughout most of its range, including Britain.

Ground-ivy *Glechoma hederacea* Up to 50cm

Rather variable, mat-forming plant not always flowering freely. A creeping, rooting, hairy perennial which is often purple-tinged. The opposite, stalked, nearly orbicular to kidney-shaped leaves are up to 35 to 40mm across. Ascending shoots usually bear pairs of pale violet flowers in the axils of leaf-like bracts. The corollas are 15 to 22mm long, with purple spots on the lower lip. Flowers from March to June and occurs almost throughout Europe including Britain. It grows in a wide variety of habitats including woodland, hedgerows and sparse grassland. In suitable sites, it sometimes grows in great profusion.

● Selfheal *Prunella vulgaris* Up to 50cm

Thought to have healing properties, this distinctive grassland herb is a creeping, mat-forming perennial with upright flowering stems. Opposite leaves are ovate to diamond-shaped, sometimes bluntly toothed and up to 5cm long. The deep violet-blue, two-lipped flowers are 13 to 15mm long, carried together with purplish bracts in dense, shortly cylindrical, terminal heads with a pair of leaves directly below. The bracts persist after the flowers have dropped. Flowers from March to November and occurs throughout most of Europe, growing along grassy, woodland rides, in meadows and on waste ground.

Marjoram *Origanum vulgare* Up to 90cm

Familiar as a culinary herb, this aromatic, erect perennial is hairy and woody at the base. Opposite leaves are ovate and 10 to 40mm long. The flowers are two-lipped, 4 to 7mm long and whitish or pale purplish-pink in colour. They are carried, together with bracts, in densely crowded, terminal heads which may be flat-topped or rather globular. Flowers from April to September and occurs across most of Europe in suitable habitats. It grows in scrub, grassland and rocky places, almost exclusively on lime-rich soils and locally common in much of its range.

Gipsywort *Lycopus europaeus* 20–120cm

Found in wet places, this species of the mint family is an erect, hairy perennial with opposite, ovate-lanceolate or elliptical leaves which are deeply pinnately lobed and 30 to 100mm long. Plant occasionally forms large clumps but more usually grows as a few stems. The white flowers are purple-spotted and about 4mm long, carried in tight whorls around the leaf nodes. The corolla has a short tube and four lobes, the uppermost being broadest. Flowers from June to September and is found across most of Europe including Britain. A wetland plant, habitats include ponds, wet ditches and marshes.

Corn Mint *Mentha arvensis* Up to 60cm

An ascending to erect, hairy perennial producing a rather acrid smell of mint when bruised. A rather variable plant, often seen around field borders. Opposite leaves vary from elliptical-lanceolate to broadly ovate and are 20 to 50mm long. The flowering stems are usually tipped with leaves. The lilac or whitish flowers are produced in dense axillary whorls. The stamens protrude noticeably from the four-lobed corollas and the calyces are 1.5 to 2.5mm long, with short, triangular teeth. Flowers from May to October and occurs throughout most of Europe on disturbed, often damp, ground.

Common Lavender *Lavandula angustifolia* Up to 100cm

A much-branched, aromatic, evergreen shrub which is familiar as a garden plant but also growing wild in southern Europe. Twigs are densely clad with lanceolate, oblong or linear leaves; these are 20 to 40mm long, are initially white-hairy but later become green. The lavender-blue or purplish, two-lipped flowers are 10 to 12mm long. They are crowded into dense, narrowly cylindrical spikes which are 20 to 80mm long and carried at the tips of long, slender and almost leafless stems. Flowers from June to September and has a widespread distribution in the Mediterannean region. It grows on dry, stony hillsides.

Rosemary *Rosmarinus officinalis* Up to 200cm

Cultivated as a culinary herb but native to southern Europe. A much-branched, aromatic, evergreen shrub with opposite, linear, leathery leaves, 15 to 40mm long, dark green on the upper surface and white-hairy beneath. Pale blue flowers are 10 to 12mm long, carried in spike-like axillary clusters; the upper lip of the corolla is very concave and there are two stamens. In its natural range, it can be found in flower at almost any time of year. It is native to the Mediterranean region but planted elsewhere in southern Europe for its aromatic oil. The plant grows in areas of dry scrub.

Meadow Clary *Salvia pratensis* Up to 100cm

A typical meadow flower in southern Europe, this erect, branching, hairy perennial has opposite and long-stalked leaves. These are ovate or ovate-oblong and wrinkled; the toothed basal leaves are 70 to 150mm long while the upper leaves are smaller and stalkless. Violet-blue flowers are 20 to 30mm long and carried in whorls of four to six in narrow terminal spikes. The corolla has a sickle-shaped, hooded upper lip and a spreading lower lip. Flowers during June and July. It occurs across most of Europe but in Britain it is rare and confined to southern England. Grows in grassland and hedges on lime-rich soils.

Henbane *Hyoscyamus niger* 30–80cm

An extremely poisonous member of the nightshade family. A stickily hairy annual or biennial with erect, branching stems. Leaves are orbicular-ovate and 150 to 200mm long; those on the stems are stalkless and clasping while the lower ones are stalked. Pale yellow flowers are funnel-shaped, 20 to 30mm across and usually have purple veins and throat. Flowers from May to September and occurs throughout most of Europe except the far north. It is locally common although its appearance in an area is rather unpredictable. The plant grows on waste ground and fallow fields, often in areas with nutrient-enriched soils.

Bittersweet *Solanum dulcamara* 30–200cm

Also known as Woody Nightshade, Bittersweet is a scrambling, branching perennial with stems becoming woody. Leaves are ovate, heart- or arrow-shaped and pointed; they are 50 to 90mm long and sometimes pinnately cut into a few lobes at the base. Dark purple flowers, 10 to 15mm across are carried in loose, branching sprays of 10 to 25. Corollas have five, recurved, lanceolate petal lobes, the yellow anthers forming a conical, central column. Shiny, juicy and ovoid berries are 10 to 15mm long and ripen red. Flowers from May to September and occurs across most of Europe in damp woodlands, hedges and waste areas.

Monkeyflower *Mimulus guttatus* Up to 50cm

Although not native to the region this species is widely naturalised. A creeping perennial with ascending or upright, hollow stems. Opposite leaves are ovate, blunt-tipped and toothed, the lowest ones being stalked. Flowers are 40 x 30mm, two-lipped and wth small red spots in the throat; they are carried on stalks in a three- to seven-flowered spike. Flowers from June to September. It is native to North America but is widely naturalised in Europe beside streams and other watery habitats. MUSK (*Mimulus moschatus*) is smaller, stickily hairy and also widely naturalised in Europe in damp habitats.

Great Mullein *Verbascum thapsus* Up to 200cm

A strikingly tall plant, often seen along roadside verges. Also known as Aaron's Rod, it is a biennial, covered with a dense white or greyish down. Basal leaves are up to 500mm and elliptical in outline. Stem leaves have stalks running down on to the winged stems. Flowers are 12 to 35mm across, yellow and more-or-less flat, carried in a crowded spike which is almost always unbranched. Flowers from June to August and occurs across most of Europe except for the far north and much of the Balkans. Typically grows in open scrub and dry, bare places and is common throughout much of its range.

Dark Mullein *Verbascum nigrum* Up to 100cm

An attractive waste-ground flower, this is a sparsely hairy perennial with ridged stems. Basal leaves are dark green, ovate to oblong, heart-shaped at the base and with a wavy margin. Flowers are 18 to 25mm across, yellow, and carried in a short-branched spike, with linear bracts 4 to 15mm long. The flower centres look dark due to the stamens being covered with violet hairs. Flowers from June to September and occurs in northern and central Europe from England, Scandinavia and northern Russia southwards to northern Spain, Italy and Greece. Grows on grassy places and well-drained chalky soil.

Water Figwort *Scrophularia auriculata* Up to 100cm

The maturing seed capsules of this small-flowered perennial resemble miniature figs. It has winged stems and is occasionally downy. Opposite leaves are 50 to 250mm long and ovate to elliptical. There are two small, toothed lobes at the base. The two-lipped flowers are 5 to 9mm across and greenish with purple-brown upper lips; they are carried in branched spikes with linear bracts. The toothed calyx lobes have broad, papery margins. Flowers from June to September and occurs from western Europe eastwards to Germany, Italy and Crete growing beside ponds and rivers. COMMON FIGWORT (*Scrophularia nodosa*) is similar but with unwinged stems.

• Common Toadflax *Linaria vulgaris* Up to 90cm

An attractive flower, similar to cultivated, garden toadflaxes. A greyish, more-or-less hairless perennial which is occasionally branched. Alternate leaves are linear, elliptical or linear-lanceolate, and crowded. Flowers are two-lipped, 25 to 35mm across and pale to bright yellow; the lower lip is orange-spotted and the stout spur is 10 to 13mm long. The flowers are carried in a dense spike. Flowers from June to October and occurs across most of Europe apart from the far north and much of the Mediterranean region. It grows on bare soils on waste ground, cultivated fields and roadside verges.

Ivy-leaved Toadflax *Cymbalaria muralis* Up to 60cm

A charming and delicate climbing plant which is often seen clambering up old, shady walls. A trailing perennial, with ivy-like, five- to nine-lobed leaves, the lobes being triangular. The two-lipped flowers are 9 to 15mm across and lilac or violet with a yellow spot; there is a 1.5 to 3mm spur and the flowers are solitary and carried on long stalks from the leaf axils. Flowers from April to October. It is widely naturalised throughout much of Europe, including Britain, but its native range includes the southern Alps, western Yugoslavia, Italy and Sicily. The plant grows on walls and banks.

Foxglove *Digitalis purpurea* Up to 180cm

The bell-shaped flowers make this one of western Europe's most distinctive plants. A downy-hairy biennial or perennial, with long-stalked, ovate or lanceolate, softly hairy basal leaves. The flowers are 40 to 55mm long and weakly two-lipped; they are purple, pale pink or sometimes white and usually black spotted on the inside. They are carried in tall, many-flowered spikes and are popular with insects such as bumblebees. Flowers from June to September and has a native range covering most of western Europe; it is also grown as an ornamental and medicinal plant. Grows in woodland clearings, scrub and heath.

Heath Speedwell *Veronica officinalis* Up to 50cm

A pretty, low-growing plant which produces delicate spikes of typical speedwell flowers. A creeping, hairy perennial with opposite leaves which are ovate to elliptical, softly hairy and toothed; the leaves are carried on 2 to 6mm stalks. Flowers are 8mm across, lilac-blue and veined; they are carried in a dense, terminal spike, each flower comprising four, equal sepal lobes and four unequal petal lobes. Flowers from May to August and occurs across most of Europe including Britain; it is common and widespread throughout most of its range. Grows in woodlands and on dry, heathy areas.

Blue Water-speedwell *Veronica anagallis-aquatica* Up to 100cm

One of several similar speedwells growing in wet places, this species is a usually hairless perennial which is often branched at the base. Opposite leaves are 20 to 100mm long, light green and ovate to ovate-lanceolate in outline; the lower ones are often stalked while the upper ones are stalkless. Flowers are 5 to 10mm across with a blue, usually four-lobed corolla veined with violet; they are carried in stalked spikes in the axils of the upper leaves. Flowers from June to August and occurs throughout Europe except the far north. It can usually be found growing beside rivers and streams.

Common Field Speedwell *Veronica persica* Up to 50cm

This extremely common speedwell of cultivated land is an attractive weed. A sprawling, hairy and branched annual it has broad, ovate leaves which are pale green and short-stalked. Flowers are 8 to 12mm across, bright blue and solitary, carried on stalks 5 to 30mm long, from the leaf axils. The corolla is unequally four-lobed. The fruit capsule has prominent ridges on the outer edges. Flowers throughout the year but less frequently in the winter months. In all likelihood, it is not native to the region, its native range being south-western Asia. Naturalised throughout Europe, mostly on bare, cultivated land.

97

Field Cow-wheat *Melampyrum arvense* Up to 60cm

Formerly a locally common cornfield weed, but now much scarcer. An impressive, hemiparasitic annual with opposite, linear or lanceolate, untoothed leaves. Two-lipped flowers are 20 to 25mm long, purple but with the lower lip and throat yellow. They are carried in a cylindrical spike with long, slender-toothed, ovate-lanceolate bracts which are green, white or reddish-pink. Flowers from June to September. It has a rather patchy distribution from Britain, where it is rare in southern England, and Finland, southwards to Spain, Italy and Turkey. The plant grows in grassland and arable fields.

Eyebright *Euphrasia nemorosa* Up to 40cm

An extremely variable grassland plant, often split into an array of species. An upright, hemiparasitic annual, with up to nine pairs of ascending branches. The mostly opposite leaves are ovate, deeply veined and toothed. The two-lipped flowers are 5 to 8.5mm across and white to lilac; they are carried in terminal spikes. Fruit capsule is 4 to 6mm long, oblong to elliptical and more than twice as long as wide. Flowers from June to October and occurs across northern and central Europe, and southwards to north-eastern Spain. It grows in grass places of all sorts and occasionally in open woodland.

Red Bartsia *Odontites verna* Up to 50cm

Despite being fairly tall, an easily overlooked plant, often seen on tracks and paths. A downy-hairy, often purple-tinged, hemiparasitic annual, with lanceolate, toothed and opposite leaves. The two-lipped flowers are 8 to 10mm long and reddish-pink; they are almost stalkless and are carried in a loose, one-sided spike that often droops slightly towards the tip. Flowers from June to September and occurs across most of Europe including Britain where it is common throughout. It is a plant of grassland, waste ground, roadsides, tracks and fields, often growing on surprisingly compacted soil.

Yellow Bartsia *Parentucellia viscosa* Up to 70cm

Often seen near the coast, this delicate and attractive plant is a stickily hairy, hemiparasitic annual. Plant is upright with oblong to lanceolate, pointed and roughly-toothed leaves. The two-lipped flowers are 16 to 24mm across and rich yellow; the lower lip is three-lobed and the flowers are carried in a loose-flowered spike. The bracts are leaf-like and the calyx lobes are lanceolate. Flowers from June to September. It occurs from southern and western Europe northwards to Scotland. Grows in damp, sandy and grassy places, and is typical of wet dune slacks in coastal sand dune.

Lousewort *Pedicularis sylvatica* Up to 25cm

An compact and attractive plant of nutrient-poor, wet acid soils. A more-or-less hairless, hemiparasitic perennial which is highly branched from the base. Leaves are usually alternate and are roughly triangular in outline, lanceolate or linear and pinnately-lobed, the lobes oblong and toothed. Flowers are pink or red, the upper, hooded lips have two teeth. The calyx is slightly two-lipped, with unequal lobes. Flowers from April to July and grows across western and central Europe to Sweden. It grows on wet heaths and bogs, and in damp, acid grassland. It is said to provide an indication of poor grazing.

Yellow-rattle *Rhinanthus minor* Up to 50cm

Distinctive both when in bloom and fruit this attractive meadow flower has seeds that rattle inside the fruit capsule. A hemiparasitic annual which is often branched and may be hairy or hairless. Leaves are opposite, linear to ovate, and toothed. Two-lipped flowers are 13 to 15mm long and have a straight corolla. The bracts are longer or only slightly shorter than the usually hairless calyx which inflates in fruit. Flowers from May to September and occurs across most of Europe, although it is rare in the Mediterranean. Grows in rough, grassy places and is often common in suitable habitats.

Toothwort *Lathraea squamaria* Up to 30cm

This easily recognisable plant of early spring is a creamy-white, pink- or orange-tinged perennial. Plant lacks chlorophyll and is parasitic on tree roots, especially those of Hazel. Stems are stout with leaves reduced to alternate, triangular scales which clasp the stem. The two-lipped flowers are 14 to 20mm long, pinkish-tinged and two-lipped; carried in a dense, one-sided spike which also bears thin, almost leaf-like bracts. Flowers during April and May and occurs across much of Europe. Distribution is rather patchy and the plant is absent from parts of the north and south. Tooth-wort grows in woods and hedges.

Knapweed Broomrape *Orobanche elatior* Up to 70cm

A tall and stately broom-rape, this species is a parasite with an un-branched, usually glan-dular-hairy stem. The scale-like leaves are 10 to 20mm long and triangu-lar-lanceolate. Flowers are two-lipped, 12 to 25mm long and are car-ried in a dense spike. The corolla is yellow and often tinged pinkish; it is downcurved, the upper lip often two-lobed, the lower one with three equal lobes. The bracts are 15 to 25mm long and lanceolate. Flowers from June to August. It occurs from England eastwards across central Europe and southwards to Spain, northern Italy and Bulgaria, typically on chalky soil.

Common Butterwort *Pinguicula vulgaris* Up to 20cm

Distinctive and unusual insectivorous plant of boggy habitats. A perennial with a rosette of yellow-green leaves which are sticky on the upper surface and trap insects which are then covered, and subsequently digested, by the leaf rolling up. The two-lipped flowers are 15 to 22mm across and violet with white at the throat; they have a straight spur, 3 to 10mm long, and are carried singly on tall, leafless spikes. Flowers from May to July and occurs across northern, central and western Europe. It grows on wet rocks, bogs and heathland, but also more occasionally on calcareous fens.

Sea Plantain *Plantago maritima* Up to 25cm

Usually found growing around the shores of Europe, this coastal plant has a rather woody base from which several rosettes of linear, fleshy leaves are produced; these are three- to five-veined and sometimes slightly toothed. The plant produces numerous flower stalks on which fairly loose, cylindrical spikes of flowers, 25 to 55mm long, are carried. Each individual flower comprises oval bracts, a brown corolla and yellow stamens. Sea Plantain flowers from June to September and can be found on coasts around most of Europe. It is typically found growing on cliffs and saltmarshes but also rarely occurs on mountains inland.

Ribwort Plantain *Plantago lanceolata* Up to 60cm

Abundant wayside plant which occurs in a wide variety of habitats. A perennial which often produces several rosettes of linear-lanceolate, three- to seven-veined, hairless or downy leaves, 20 to 300mm long. The flowers are small, brownish and carried in a short, dense, terminal spike on a long, deeply-furrowed stalk. Flowers from April to October and occurs throughout most of Europe except the far north. It can be found in waste places, grassland, roadside verges and in cultivated fields. It is common throughout its range and often a major component plant in meadows.

Twinflower *Linnaea borealis* Up to 50cm

This charming and aptly-named plant of northern and upland forests is a mat-forming, evergreen dwarf shrub with slender stems. Leaves are ovate and toothed. Flowers are 5 to 9mm long, bell-shaped but spreading and pinkish-white; the inside of the flower is hairy and they are carried in pairs on a single, glandular-hairy stalk, 45 to 80mm long. Flowers from June to August. It is widespread in northern Europe, and very locally common in Scotland, but becoming scarce and scattered in mountains southwards to the Alps and eastern Carpathians. Grows in woods and on heaths and tundra in the far north.

Honeysuckle *Lonicera periclymenum* Up to 600cm

A familiar sweet-scented woodland and hedgerow plant which sometimes grows in gardens. It is a vigorous, woody, deciduous climber with oblong to elliptical leaves which are dark green above but greyish-green below. Fresh leaves often appear as early as January. Flowers are carried in long-stalked terminal heads. The corolla is 35 to 55mm long, yellow or sometimes creamy-white, often red-tinged, with a long tube and two lips. Fruits are red, juicy berries. Flowers from June to October and occurs in western, central and southern Europe, north-eastwards to southern Sweden. It grows profusely in hedges and woodland borders, and rather less vigorously in woodland interiors.

Red Valerian *Centranthus ruber* Up to 80cm

A colourful flower, popular with pollinating insects and gardeners alike. A hairless, grey-green perennial which is usually branched and upright. Opposite leaves are ovate to lanceolate and pointed; the upper ones are irregularly toothed and clasping the stem. Tubular, five-lobed flowers are 5 to 10mm long, pink, white or red with a 2 to 12mm long spur; they are carried in several oblong clusters together forming a terminal head. Flowers from May to September. Its native range includes most of the Mediterranean but it is widely naturalised as far north as Britain, growing on walls and rocky places.

Teasel *Dipsacus fullonum* Up to 200cm

A hairless biennial with stout stems, prickly on the angles. Basal leaves are elliptical or oblong-lanceolate, rough and untoothed. Stem leaves are narrower, often joined around the stem and collecting water. Individual flowers are small and pale purple, and carried in a globular to egg-shaped, spiny head, 30 to 90mm across; two or three rows of upcurved, linear bracts arise at the base, the longest as long as the head. The flowers often open only two or three rows at a time. Flowers during July and August and occurs in southern, western and central Europe. It is a plant of waste ground.

Devil's-bit Scabious *Succisa pratensis* Up to 100cm

Considered by herbalists to have healing properties for the skin, this compact-flowered plant of damp, grassy places is a more-or-less downy, upright perennial with narrowly obovate or elliptical basal leaves that are sometimes slightly toothed. Flowers are 4 to 7mm across, purple, pinkish or white and carried in a dense, round head 15 to 30mm across. Male and female flowers are produced on different heads, the female being smaller. Flowers from June to October and occurs across most of Europe except for the far north and parts of the Mediterranean. Grows in damp meadows and woodlands.

105

Small Scabious *Scabiosa columbaria* Up to 70cm

Formerly used to treat scabies this typical chalk grassland flower is a branched, downy perennial with basal rosettes of entire or pinnately-lobed leaves. Stem leaves are pinnately-lobed, the lobes themselves also being pinnate and roughly hairy. Individual flowers are bluish-lilac and are carried in a head, 15 to 25mm across; beneath the flower head is a ruff of green bracts. Flowers from June to October. It ranges from southern Scotland to Estonia and southwards through central Europe. Grows in dry grassland, usually on limestone or chalk and is locally common in suitable habitats throughout its range.

● Nettle-leaved Bellflower *Campanula trachelium* Up to 100cm

This attractive plant is one of the showiest members of the bell-flower family. It is a bristly-hairy perennial with angled stems. Leaves are ovate to heart-shaped, pointed and toothed; the lower ones are stalked. Flowers are bell-shaped with spreading tips, 15 to 50mm long and pale blue or violet; they are carried in a leafy spike. The calyx teeth are triangular and pointed. Flowers from July to September. It occurs across much of central Europe, northwards to Sweden and is very locally common in southern England. It is a plant of woodland rides, scrubby grassland and hedgerows.

Harebell *Campanula rotundifolia* Up to 70cm

One of the best known and commonly widespread members of the bellflower family, this perennial has creeping stems that abruptly become erect. Basal leaves are rounded, 6 to 12mm across and carried on stalks. Nodding, bell-shaped flowers are 10 to 30mm long, blue and solitary or carried in a loose spike. The calyx teeth are linear to narrowly triangular. Flowers from June to October and occurs across much of Europe although it is rare in the south. It is found on dry grassland and heath, sand dunes and rocks. Grows on both acid and calcareous soils and is common throughout much of its range.

Round-headed Rampion *Phyteuma orbiculare* Up to 50cm

A distinctive and attractive plant of chalk grassland. This upright, unbranched perennial has basal leaves that are linear-lanceolate or elliptical, toothed and stalked. The unusually shaped, individual flowers are small, blue or blue-violet; up to 30 are carried in a dense, globular head 10 to 25mm across with a ring of ovate-lanceolate, pointed bracts beneath. Flowers from June to August. It is very local in southern England but is more widespread across central Europe to Latvia and southwards to southern Spain and Albania. The plant can be found growing in dry grassland, almost always on chalky soils.

Sheep's-bit *Jasione montana* Up to 50cm

Superficially similar to Devil's-bit Scabious, this is a plant of dry, lime-free soils. This upright, slightly hairy annual or biennial has wavy-edged, linear-oblong to lanceolate leaves; these are produced in a basal rosette. Flowers are small, blue and carried in a globular head beneath which is a ruff of bracts. Flowers are 5mm long and bear stamens that do not protrude. This lack of protrudence is the easiest way to distinguish this plant from scabiouses. Flowers from May to September and occurs across most of Europe as far north as Finland. It is a plant of dry grassland, heaths and coastal rock and shingle.

Hemp Agrimony *Eupatorium cannabinum* Up to 175cm

Often seen growing beside fresh water, this large, showy plant is an upright, often reddish, downy perennial with three- to five-lobed leaves. Lobes themselves are ovate to lanceolate, pointed and toothed. The florets are small, in pinkish clusters 2-5mm across; these are gathered together in a terminal head. The seeds have a parachute of white hairs and are wind dispersed. Flowers from July to September and occurs across most of Europe. It is most typically a plant of damp places such as riversides and fens but occasionally grows in drier situations. Locally common throughout most of its range.

Goldenrod *Solidago virgaurea* Up to 100cm

Formerly used as a wound-herb this rather variable, autumn-flowering plant is a mostly downy perennial, with oblanceolate to obovate leaves which are downy underneath. The flower heads are yellow and carried in branched spikes. Individual heads are 5 to 10mm across and comprise 10 to 30 disc florets, each surrounded by six to twelve ray florets. Seeds are wind dispersed and have a 5mm long parachute of hairs. Flowers from June to September and occurs across most of Europe. Grows in a wide variety of habitats such as woods, heaths and grassy and rocky places. Locally common in much of its range.

Daisy *Bellis perennis* Up to 25cm

A familiar sight on lawns and meadows. A spreading perennial with spoon-shaped, slightly toothed leaves narrowing abruptly to the stalk; these are produced in a flat rosette. Flower heads are 15 to 30mm across, solitary and carried on a slender stalk. The disc florets are yellow and the white ray florets are sometimes reddish on the back; the flowers close at night and in dull weather. Seeds are hairless. Usually in flower throughout the year although the peak for flowering is between April and October. It occurs across most of Europe on grassy places and roadsides.

109

Blue Fleabane *Erigeron acer* Up to 100cm

A common but easily overlooked plant of well-drained soils, this densely hairy annual is biennial or perennial with spoon-shaped, stalked basal leaves that are up to 70mm long; the stem leaves are unstalked and lanceolate. The flower heads are 10 to 15mm across with up to 70 in a terminal cluster. The disc florets are yellow while the ray florets are lilac and erect. Blue Fleabane flowers from July to September and occurs across most of Europe, although its precise distribution is rather patchy. It grows on dry, stony or sandy places, often on bare soil; sand dunes and stable shingle beaches offer ideal conditions.

Marsh Cudweed *Gnaphalium uliginosum* Up to 30cm

A plant which often thrives in damp cart ruts, tracks and marshy places. This much branched, silvery hairy annual can be both ascending or spreading depending on the location. Flower heads are dull yellow, 4mm long and carried in terminal clusters of 3 to 10, often seemingly shrouded by the long leaves at their base. Flowers from July to September and occurs across most of Europe as far north as southern Scandinavia. Grows in damp habitats of all kinds such as pond margins, woodland rides and paths. Common throughout most of its range and sometimes abundant in suitable conditions.

Edelweiss *Leontopodium alpinum* Up to 30cm

This classic mountain plant, beloved of botanists and alpine gardeners alike, is difficult to confuse with any other plant. An upright perennial which is densely white-hairy and has obovate to oblong leaves with smooth margins. Flower heads comprise small yellowish-white disc florets which are globular, in dense clusters and with a whorl of leaves beneath; the involucral bracts are densely hairy. Flowers from July to September. It grows in rocky, grassy places in mountains of mainland Europe and is more-or-less restricted to areas of limestone. Very locally common in the Alps.

Golden Samphire *Inula crithmoides* Up to 100cm

An autumn visit to the coast can be worth it just to see a display of this plant. A hairless perennial which is often woody at the base and has fleshy, linear leaves that are usually three-toothed at the apex. Flower heads up to 25mm across, florets yellow and comprise 14 to 25 ray florets which are longer than the bracts. Flowers from July to October and occurs around the coasts of southern and western Europe; it is also found inland in eastern Spain. It typically grows on saltmarshes, shingles beaches and cliffs. In some areas, particularly certain estuaries, it forms extensive stands.

Common Fleabane *Pulicaria dysenterica* Up to 60cm

An attractive, wayside member of the daisy family whose leaves were formerly used for insecticidal properties. A branched, woolly-hairy perennial with leaves oblong-lanceolate, wavy-edged and green above but greyish-woolly beneath. The short-stalked flower heads are 15 to 30mm across and carried in loose clusters. Both the disc and ray florets are yellow and the involucral bracts are linear or pointed. Flowers from July to September and occurs from southern, western and central Europe northwards to Denmark. It grows in damp places and is common in Britain except northern Scotland. The leaves were formerly used for their insecticidal properties.

Corn Chamomile *Anthemis arvensis* Up to 80cm

One of the most colourful and distinctive cornfield weeds. Corn Chamomile is a usually branched, greyish, downy-hairy annual or biennial. Leaves are much divided into linear segments, each with a bristle-like point, and the whole plant is aromatic. Flower heads are 15 to 40mm across, solitary, and carried at the tips of branches. The disc florets are yellow while the ray florets are white. The involucral bracts are hairy and usually oblong, with brown papery margins. Flowers from April to October and occurs across much of Europe including southern England. A weed of cultivation and typically grows on chalky soils.

Yarrow *Achillea millefolium* Up to 60cm

A strongly aromatic, wayside plant, this upright, downy perennial has much-divided dark green leaves, the final segments of which are ovate to lanceolate, or linear. Flower heads are up to 10mm across and carried in flat-topped clusters. Disc florets are creamy white while the ray florets are white or pink and five in number. Flowers from June to November and occurs across much of Europe; it is widespread in Britain but rare in the Mediterranean region. It grows in grassland, waste places and roadside verges, especially as a turf weed. Generally common throughout the whole of its range.

Sea Mayweed *Tripleurospermum maritimum* Up to 80cm

Superficially similar to other mayweed species but exclusively a maritime plant. A prostrate or upright, branched perennial. The leaves are much divided, the segments being short and fleshy and either blunt or with a bristle-like point. The disc florets are yellow and the ray florets are white. Flowers from April to October and occurs in coastal areas of western and northern Europe. It typically grows on bare areas such as stabilised shingle beaches. SCENT-LESS MAYWEED (*Tripleurospermum inodorum*) is similar but has leaf segments which are not fleshy. A common plant of cultivated and waste ground throughout Europe.

113

Crown Daisy *Chrysanthemum coronarium* Up to 80cm

An attractive wayside flower of southern Europe which is an ascending or upright, usually hairless annual. Leaves are usually pinnately-lobed, the lobes divided into oblong or lanceolate, toothed segments. Flower heads are 30 to 50mm across and solitary on the tips of stalks. The disc and ray florets are yellow. The involucral bracts are ovate with a brown band, white papery margin and papery appendages. Flowers from April to July. It is widespread in central and southern Portugal and throughout the Mediterranean region, occasionally being naturalised elsewhere. The plant grows on waste places and cultivated ground.

Corn Marigold *Chrysanthemum segetum* Up to 80cm

Sometimes growing in sufficient profusion to turn fields yellow, this colourful cornfield weed is a bluish-green, rather fleshy annual. Leaves are usually oblong, the middle and lower stem leaves being deeply toothed; the upper leaves are mostly entire and clasp the stem. Flower heads are 35 to 55mm across, bright golden yellow and solitary at the tips of stems. Flowers from June to October. Probably native only to the Aegean region, the plant has been extensively naturalised in western and parts of northern Europe including Britain. Grows mainly on acid soils, and its numbers fluctuate greatly from year to year.

Tansy *Tanacetum vulgare* Up to 150cm

This aromatic herb with medicinal and insecticidal properties is a strong-smelling perennial, branched towards the top. The leaves are glandular and pinnately lobed, the segments further lobed or divided; the lower leaves are stalked. The flower heads are 5 to 10mm across and yellow, with up to 100 carried in a dense, flat-topped cluster resembling an umbel. Only disc florets are present in the flower heads. Tansy flowers from July to October and occurs across most of Europe. It grows in grassland waste places, often as an escape from cultivation. The plant is common throughout most of its range.

Oxeye Daisy *Leucanthemum vulgare* Up to 100cm

A familiar and widespread wayside plant with typical daisy-like flowers. A perennial which is little if at all branched. The leaves are dark grey-green, the basal ones being obovate or spoon-shaped, long-stalked and gently toothed; the stem leaves are stalkless and deeply lobed. The flower heads are 20 to 90mm across and usually solitary; the disc florets are yellow while the ray florets are white. The involucral bracts are ovate to lanceolate, with a dark, papery margin. Flowers from May to September and occurs across most of Europe including Britain. It grows in grassy places and is common throughout most of its range.

Mugwort *Artemisia vulgaris* Up to 150cm

Used in herbal remedies for treating liver complaints, this aromatic plant is a tufted perennial whose stems are often red- or purple-tinged. Leaves are stalkless and pinnately lobed, the segments occasionally also deeply lobed; the leaves are dark green and hairless above, densely woolly-hairy beneath. Flower heads are yellowish, 1.5 to 3.5mm across, ovoid and carried numerously in branched spikes; disc florets only are present. The involucral bracts are greyish and downy-hairy. Flowers from July to September and occurs across most of Europe except the far north and south. It grows on roadsides and waste places.

Colt's-foot *Tussilago farfara* Up to 15cm

Best known for its spikes of flowers produced in early spring, this wayside plant is a perennial which flowers well before the large, round, shallowly-lobed and toothed leaves emerge. Leaves themselves are green above, white-woolly beneath and up to 300mm across when mature. Flower heads are 15 to 35mm across, solitary and carried on a stem with purple scales; both the disc and narrow ray florets are bright yellow. Fruiting head is nodding. Flowers from February to April and occurs across most of Europe including Britain. Grows in damp, wet places, often on bare soil that has beendisturbed recently.

116

Butterbur *Petasites hybridus* Up to 30cm

A showy, early-spring flower of waterside habitats. A distinctive perennial which flowers before the leaves emerge. Leaves are up to 100cm across, heart-shaped and downy-grey beneath; the margins bear irregular, blunt teeth. Flower heads are unisexual and lilac or yellowish in colour. Sixty to 130 heads are carried on each purplish-scaled stem; those of the male plants are 60 to 85mm across while those of female plants are 30 to 65mm across. Flowers from March to May and occurs across much of Europe northwards to Britain, Germany and central Russia. Grows in damp places, especially streamsides.

Leopard's-bane *Doronicum pardalianches* Up to 70cm

One of several similar species growing wild in Europe but also popular as a garden plant. An upright, downy perennial with ovate to heart-shaped basal leaves. Upper leaves are lanceolate and with shorter stalks up the stem. Flower heads are 35 to 50mm across and carried in loose, clusters of two to five heads. Both the disc and ray florets are bright yellow. Flowers during July and August and has a scattered distribution in central and western Europe as far north as Holland. In Britain it is naturalised locally and has a patchy distribution. Grows in woodland rides and on grassy verges.

Ragwort *Senecio jacobaea* Up to 150cm

Often covered with the orange-and-black striped caterpillars of the Cinnabar Moth, this is a common and often invasive plant of waste ground. Stout, often hairless biennial or perennial which is branched at the top. Leaves are pinnately lobed, the terminal lobes being blunt; the stem leaves clasp the stem and are sparsely hairy beneath while the lower leaves are stalked. Flower heads are 15 to 20mm across, yellow and numerous in dense clusters. There are 12 to 15 ray florets. Flowers from June to November and occurs across most of Europe although it is rare in the north. Grows in dry grassy and waste places.

Carline Thistle *Carlina vulgaris* Up to 70cm

An unusual downland plant whose flowers look dead and dried at all times. An upright, hairless or downy biennial with leaves that are linear-oblong to ovate and spiny-toothed. Flower heads 15 to 30mm across and yellowish-brown; solitary or carried in groups of two or three. Flower heads comprise disc florets only but are surrounded by long, lanceolate, involucral bracts that are yellowish and resemble ray florets; there are also spiny, outer bracts that are greenish. Flowers from July to September and occurs across most of Europe. Grows in grassy and stony places, usually on chalky soils.

118

Lesser Burdock *Arctium minus* Up to 150cm

A common plant of waste ground, this downy biennial has broadly ovate basal leaves which are heart-shaped at the base and have hollow leaf stalks. Flower heads are 15 to 30mm across, ovoid and solitary or in short-stalked clusters of purple disc florets only. The outer involucral bracts, which cover the swollen base of the flower head, end in long, hooked spines. In seed, these become caught in animal fur, thus aiding their dispersal. Flowers from July to September and occurs throughout Europe except the Arctic. It grows in waste places and on roadside verges.

Musk Thistle *Carduus nutans* Up to 150cm

Also known as Nodding Thistle on account of its slightly drooping flower heads, this thistle is a perennial with white, cottony, winged stems, the wings with spiny, triangular lobes. Leaves have six to ten pairs of spine-tipped lobes. Flower heads are 20 to 45mm across and usually solitary. The flower heads comprise reddish-purple disc florets only; the involucral bracts are spine-tipped, the uppermost ones being bent back. Flowers from June to September and occurs across western and central Europe, northwards to Scotland and southwards to Sicily and Yugoslavia. Grows in bare and grassy places.

Spear Thistle *Cirsium vulgare* Up to 300cm

Famous as the emblem of Scottish kings, this attractive and vigorous weed of waste places is a downy biennial with winged, spiny stems. Leaves are pinnately lobed, spiny and sparsely cottony-hairy or downy underneath; the leaf bases run down onto the stem. Flower heads are 20 to 40mm across. The purple florets are all disc florets; the involucral bracts narrow into sharp spines covering the swollen base of the flower head. Flowers from July to September and occurs throughout most of Europe including Britain. It grows in waste places and on bare and disturbed ground. Common and persistant across much of its range.

Stemless Thistle *Cirsium acaule* Up to 35cm

Also known as Dwarf Thistle, this plant is painfully familiar to anyone who has attempted to sit on a downland slope. A perennial which is usually stemless with wavy-edged leaves are produced in a basal rosette, oblong-lanceolate and pinnately lobed. Lobes are ovate or semi-circular in outline, toothed and spiny. Flower heads are 20 to 50mm across and solitary; the purple florets are all disc and the involucral bracts have spiny tips. Flowers from June to September and occurs from England across central Europe to Estonia and south to Spain and Yugoslavia growing on lime-rich soils.

Red Star-thistle *Centaurea calcitrapa* Up to 100cm

An extremely spiny wayside plant which is an ascending or upright perennial, much-branched from the base. Leaves are grey-woolly when young, becoming greenish or downy. Lower leaves are pinnately-lobed and usually wither early; the upper ones have linear-lanceolate, spiny lobes. Flower heads are 8 to 10mm across, stalk-less, surrounded by the upper leaves. The pale purple florets are all disc and the involucral bracts end in a long, yellow spine. Flowers from July to September. Occurs in southern and south-central Europe but it is naturalised in western and central Europe including southern England. Grows in dry, waste places.

Common Knapweed *Centaurea nigra* Up to 100cm

Also known as Hard-heads this is an erect or ascending, branched perennial. The leaves are green to grey and cottony-hairy; the lower leaves are lanceolate to ovate and toothed or lobed, while the upper leaves are lanceolate and entire. Flower heads are 20 to 40mm across and solitary or in clusters at the tips of branches. Flowers are purple and all disc florets; the involucral bracts have black or blackish-brown apical appendages. Flowers from June to September and is widespread in Europe as far north-east as Sweden and as far south-east as Italy. It grows in grassland and hedges.

121

Greater Knapweed *Centaurea scabiosa* Up to 90cm

A conspicuous and showy downland plant much loved by pollinating insects. This tall, erect perennial is downy and has grooved stems. The lower leaves are stalked and pinnately lobed, the lobes themselves being toothed; the upper leaves lack stalks. Flower heads are large and solitary, 30 to 55mm across; the reddish-purple florets are variable, the outer ones being very long and spreading. The involucral bracts are green. Flowers from June to August and occurs across much of Europe from central Spain, central Italy and Bulgaria northwards to southern Britain. Grows in grassy areas, mostly on chalky or limestone soils.

Bristly Oxtongue *Picris echioides* Up to 90cm

A relative of the Dandelion, this sprawling, wayside plant is a much branched annual or biennial, covered with rough, raised hairs. Basal leaves are elliptical or oblong, blunt or sharp-pointed, wavy to toothed and with a winged stalk. Lower stem leaves are similar but with the stalk clasping the stem. Upper stem leaves are lanceolate or ovate, stalkless, clasping the stem. Flower heads are 20 to 25mm across, many in a cluster and composed of yellow ray florets only. Flowers from June to November. Widespread in southern Europe but is widely naturalised north to southern Britain, growing in rough, grassy places.

Dandelion *Taraxacum officinale* Up to 50cm

Famous as an ingredient for wine, this extremely familiar flower of meadows and grassland is a very variable perennial. A basal rosette of leaves range from almost entire to deeply pinnately lobed, produced on often winged stalks. Flower heads are 35 to 50mm across and solitary at the tips of stout, hollow stalks. Flowers are composed of yellow ray florets only. Dandelion can be found in flower throughout the year although peak flowering occurs from April to June. It is widespread across most of Europe and grows in grassland and on waste ground and cultivated land. Common throughout the whole of its range. AUTUMN HAWKBIT (*Leontodon autumnalis*) is similar but nearly hairless.

Smooth Hawk's-beard *Crepis capillaris* Up to 100cm

A relative of the Dandelion this is a common grassland and wayside plant. An annual or biennial which is often many-stemmed and branched from the base. Leaves are hairless or sparsely hairy, pinnately lobed, the lobes being triangular. Stem leaves clasp the stem. Flower heads are 10 to 15mm across and are carried in loose clusters; they are composed of ray florets only, the outer often red-tinged. The outer involucral bracts are spreading. Flowers from June to November and occurs in western, central and southern Europe. It grows in grassland and waste areas and is common throughout much of its range.

123

Mouse-ear Hawkweed *Hieraceum pilosella* Up to 50cm

This small but extremely robust, grassland plant is a perennial with long, leafy stolons and a basal rosette of leaves. Leaves are oblanceolate, spoon-shaped or elliptical, blunt-tipped and with long hairs on both sides. Flower heads are 20 to 30mm across, solitary and carried at the tips of leafless stems; they are composed of ray florets only which are lemon-yellow and striped with red below. Flowers from May to October and occurs across most of Europe including Britain. Grows in grassland of all sorts including hedges, wasteground and roadside verges and is common throughout most of its range.

Common Water-plantain *Alisma plantago-aquatica* 20–100cm

Widespread and distinctive, this aquatic plant grows in shallow water. A stout aquatic perennial with aerial leaves, the first ones reduced to a narrow-bladed stalk; subsequent leaves have an ovate blade, rounded or heart-shaped at the base. Flowers are borne in a much branched cluster. All parts of the flower are in threes; the petals are 3.5 to 6.5mm across and usually pale lilac but sometimes white. Flowers open from early afternoon to evening. Flowers from June to August and occurs across most of Europe except for a few islands. Grows in still ponds, slow-moving rivers, canals and marshy places.

Bog Asphodel *Narthecium ossifragum* 5–45cm

A pretty flower of heathland bogs, this perennial plant has rigid, curved basal leaves, 30 to 150mm long, arranged in a flat fan. Stem leaves are much smaller and clasping. There is a terminal spike on which six to twenty bright yellow flowers are carried; these, with the stem, turn orange after pollination. The six spreading perianth segments are petal-like in appearance and 6 to 9mm long; the stamens are woolly. Flowers from July to September. Occurs across northwest Europe including Britain, eastwards to Sweden and the Czech Republic and southwards to Spain. Grows in acid bogs.

White False-helleborine *Veratrum album* 50–175cm

This large and distinctive plant of mountain pastures is a robust perennial with hollow, leafy stems. Leaves are alternate, the lower 100 to 250mm long, elliptical, finely hairy beneath and with a long sheathing base. Inflorescence contains numerous flowers each 15 to 25mm across. The six perianth segments are wide-spreading, greenish or yellowish, with whitish on the inside. Flowers during July and August and occurs locally across much of Europe except for Britain and the north-west, islands and parts of the north-east. It is a plant of upland meadows, hedges and woods.

Meadow Saffron *Colchicum autumnale* Up to 10cm

Appearing in the Autumn, this crocus-like flower is an erect perennial with broadly lanceolate leaves 150 to 300mm long which develop in the spring as the fruit ripens and are absent when the flowers appear. Flowers are produced; these are goblet-shaped with pale purple perianth lobes 30 to 45mm long and a paler tube 50 to 200mm long. There are six stamens. Flowers appear straight from the ground but the stalk elongates later so the ripe fruit is borne well above soil level. Flowers from August to November. Its main range covers south-west and central Europe and it is very local in England. Grows in damp meadows.

Wild Tulip *Tulipa sylvestris* 8–45cm

The most widespread tulip to be found growing wild in Europe, this bulbous perennial sometimes also produces creeping, rooting stems. Erect flowering stem has two to three narrow leaves, 30cm long, with incurved margins forming a channel. One or rarely two yellow flowers are produced and droop in bud. The three inner perianth segments are 21-70 x 6-26mm and the outer three segments are slightly shorter and narrower, sometimes tinged green, pink or crimson. Flowers from April to June. Its main range is from southern Europe north to France and central Russia but it is naturalised elsewhere. Grows in meadows.

Snake's-head Fritillary *Fritillaria meleagris* 12–50cm

This classic wet mea dow species is local but sometimes abundant in suitable sites. A slender perennial with a small bulb and a solitary, drooping flower. There are four to eight alternate, linear, bluish leaves up to 200mm long. Six perianth segments form a bell-shaped flower which is 30 to 45mm long and purple, pink or white, the outside usually with a chequerboard pattern of alternate light and dark purple squares. Flowers during April and May. It occurs from southern England to central Russia and south to the southern Alps and central Yugoslavia; naturalised elsewhere. The plant grows in damp grassland.

Martagon Lily *Lilium martagon* 30–100cm

Popular with gardeners, this extremely attractive lily is widely naturalised. A tall, bulbous perennial with whorls of oblanceolate leaves up to 160mm long. The large flowers hang down on curved stalks; they comprise six pink to purplish-red, often spotted perianth segments up to 35mm long which are strongly recurved revealing prominent stamens. Flowers from June to September and occurs from France and the Baltic south to central Spain and Greece. It is naturalised elsewhere including, locally, southern England. The plant grows in woods and grassy scrub, preferring damp soils. It is rather local.

Bluebell *Hyacinthoides non-scripta* 20–50cm

In many parts of western Europe, an abundant woodland plant in spring. A perennial with three to six leaves which are about as long as the stem and all basal. The flower spike is one-sided and drooping at the tip, with four to sixteen fragrant, hanging flowers. The cylindrical, blue perianth is 14 to 20mm long and has six segments joined at the base, their tips curving outwards; the anthers are cream. Flowers from April to June. It is native to western Europe but also naturalised in central Europe. The plant grows in woods, hedgerows and on coastal cliffs. It responds well when woodlands are coppiced, creating increased light.

Grape-hyacinth *Muscari neglectum* 4–30cm

Rather common in southern Europe, this plant of sunny, well-drained sites is a bulbous perennial with between three and six semi-cylindrical leaves 60 to 400 × 1-8mm. The dense spike has sterile upper flowers that are smaller and paler than the fertile lower ones. The perianth of the fertile flowers is dark blue, 3 to 7.5mm long; ovoid to urn-shaped with six small, whitish, recurved lobes. Flowers during April and May. Occurs across most of Europe from France and southern Russia southwards. In Britain, the plant is possibly native in a few sites but is naturalised elsewhere. Grows in dry, grassy places.

Rose Garlic *Allium roseum* 10–65cm

An attractive flower that is popular with gardeners. A perennial with bulbs producing numerous bulblets. The two to four leaves are 120 to 350mm long, linear and flat but sheathing the base of the stem. There is a terminal umbel with five to thirty flowers and up to 70mm across; this has two to four papery sheaths. The bell- to cup-shaped flowers have pink or white perianth segments which are 7 to 12mm long; the outer three are obovate while the inner three are narrowly elliptical. Flowers in June and is widespread in southern Europe; it is naturalised in Britain. The plant grows on dry, open ground.

Ramsons *Allium ursinum* 10–50cm

Carpeting woodland floors with white in the spring, this perennial has a solitary, narrow bulb and a sharply-angled stem. Two bright green leaves have a narrowly elliptical blade 60 to 250mm long, and a strongly curved stalk 50 to 200mm long. Flowers are carried in a loose, flat-topped umbel 25 to 60mm across which has six to 20 individual white flowers and two papery sheaths beneath. Flowers from April to June. Occurs across most of Europe except parts of the north-east and it is rare in the Mediterranean region. Grows on damp, lime-rich soils and is locally abundant.

Common Solomon's-seal *Polygonatum multiflorum* 15–60cm

A fairly common woodland flower of shady groves. A hairless perennial with cylindrical, curved stems, often seen growing in sizeable clumps. Alternate leaves are 120 to 150mm long, ovate and mostly stalkless. The scentless flowers are stalked and pendulous and carried in clusters of two to five. The bell-shape perianth is somewhat pinched in at the middle and greenish-white in colour. Occurs across most of Europe except parts of the south-west, east and many islands. In Britain, as elsewhere in Europe, its precise distribution is rather patchy. The plant grows in woods, often on chalky soils.

Herb-paris *Paris quadrifolia* 10–40cm

Unusual and distinctive spring woodland flower which is a perennial with a creeping rhizome and erect stems. These bear a single whorl of four to eight, obovate, stalkless leaves 50 to 160mm long at the tip. The solitary greenish flower is carried on a stalk 20 to 80mm long with four to six lanceolate sepals and four to six extremely narrow petals, all 20 to 35mm long. Flowers from May to July and occurs across most of Europe although it is rare in the Mediterranean region. In Britain, the plant is rather local but on mainland Europe it is less so. Grows in damp woods, usually on lime- or chalk-rich soils.

Summer Snowflake *Leucojum aestivum* Up to 60cm

This lovely late spring flower is a bulbous perennial with broadly linear leaves up to 300 × 5-20mm, all of which are basal. The hollow flowering stem is flattened and two-winged, with a terminal umbel of two to five flowers enclosed in bud by a papery sheath. Bell-shaped flowers hang from stalks of unequal length. The six perianth segments are 14 to 18mm long, white with a green spot at the thickened tip. Flowers from April to June and occurs south of a line from southern Ireland, England and Czechoslovakia, southwards to Sardinia and Greece. Grows in damp places and is locally common.

Snowdrop *Galanthus nivalis* Up to 25cm

This classic flower heralds spring. Its precise distribution is blurred by naturalised populations. A bulbous perennial with a single pair of bluish, linear leaves 50 to 130 × 2-7mm. Flowers are solitary and initially enclosed by a papery sheath. Perianth segments are petal-like; the outer three are 12 to 35mm long, white, the inner three 6 to 11mm long, white with a green patch at the tip. Flowers from February to March. Occurs naturally from France and Russia south to the Pyrenees, Sicily and Greece. Probably naturalised further north. Locally common in Britain. Grows in damp woodland.

131

Marsh Helleborine *Epipactis palustris* Up to 70cm

A locally common orchid of marshy habitats this creeping perennial with four to eight oblong-lanceolate, pointed leaves which decrease in size up the stem. Flowers are 15 to 20mm across, wide open, with seven to fourteen in a spike. The three sepals are purple or purple-brown; the petals are whitish and pink-tinged, the lower one being white and fringed. Flowers during July and August and occurs across most of Europe except the far north and parts of the Mediterranean. In Britain, it occurs in southern England and Wales. It is a plant of marshes and is sometimes common where it does occur.

Sword-leaved Helleborine *Cephalanthera longifolia* Up to 50cm

Also known as Narrow-leaved Helleborine, this is an unusual and attractive orchid with flowers that do not open wide. An upright perennial with long, narrow leaves, the upper ones of which are linear. The flowers are white and rather tubular, seldom opening wider than the width of the middle part of the flower; the perianth segments are pointed. Flowers are longer than the bracts and are carried in a fairly crowded spike of up to to 30 flowers. Occurs across most of Europe, including Britain where it is very local in southern England. It grows in woods and areas of shaded scrub.

Common Twayblade *Listera ovata* Up to 60cm

The leaves of this widespread orchid are somewhat more distinctive than its easily overlooked flowers. An upright perennial usually with a single pair of opposite, broadly ovate or elliptical leaves; occasionally, one or two bract-like leaves are carried further up the stem. Short-stalked flowers are up to 10mm across and carried in a loose spike. Sepals are green and the petals are yellowish-green; the top petals and sepals form a loose hood. The lip is 7 to 15mm long and two-lobed. Flowers from May to July and occurs across most of Europe including Britain in woodlands, scrub and grassland.

Autumn Lady's-tresses *Spiranthes spiralis* Up to 20cm

A charming, autumn-flowering orchid of short turf. A short perennial with the next year's basal rosette of ovate-elliptical, pointed, grey-green leaves present beside the current year's flowering stem. Flowers are 6 to 10mm long, white and scented, with six to twenty on a single spiral spike. Lateral sepals are diverging while the upper sepal and the top two petals form a tube, with the yellow-green labellum upwardly curved. Flowers during August and September and occurs across southern, western and central Europe northwards to Denmark. Grows in dry grassland, often on chalk or near the coast.

Burnt Orchid *Orchis ustulata* Up to 20cm

In its early flowering stages, an aptly-named plant, the spikes resembling glowing tubes of cigarette ash. An upright perennial with two to three oblong leaves at the base and one to three up the lower half of the stem. Flowers are carried in a dense spike, are 5 to 7mm across with a dark reddish-purple hood becoming paler with age; the lip is white or pink, purple-spotted and lobed and the spur is cylindrical and down-pointing. Flowers in May and June; a few populations appear in late July. Occurs from England to Russia and southwards to southern Europe. Grows on chalk grassland and in mountain meadows.

Lizard Orchid *Himantoglossum hircinum* Up to 90cm

An intruiging orchid with flowers fancifully resembling small lizards. A stout perennial, the stems often with faint purple blotches. Lower leaves are oval while upper ones are smaller, pointed and clasping the stem. Unusual flowers are 15 to 20mm across, greenish-grey with purple spots. Flower lip is 30 to 50mm long, with two short lateral lobes and a long central lobe; it is whitish with purple spots. Widespread and sometimes common in southern and western Europe; in Britain, it is rare and confined to the south of England. Grows on lime-rich soil in woods, grassland, scrub and dunes.

Fly Orchid *Orchis insectifera* Up to 60cm

A delicate orchid whose insect-like flowers attract small bumblebees for pollination. An upright perennial with seven to nine, linear-lanceolate, shiny leaves which are erect, pointed and carried up the stem. Flowers are 12 to 16mm across and three to fourteen in a loose spike. Sepals are green, the petals are blackish-violet and linear; the lip is furry, maroon-violet in colour, the central lobes elongated with a bluish-lilac patch at the base. Flowers in May and June and occurs across much of Europe except the south-east; local in southern Britain. Grows in woods and grassland on lime-rich soils.

Bee Orchid *Ophrys apifera* Up to 50cm

The most widespread of several similar orchid species with bumblebee-like flowers. An upright perennial with ovate-lanceolate, basal leaves and lanceolate stem leaves. Flowers are 12 to 25mm across and up to eight are carried in a loose spike. The outer perianth segments are pink and the lip is swollen and globular, and reddish-brown; it is furry with a variable yellow pattern enclosing a red patch near the base and two yellow spots near the apex. Flowers during June and July. It is widespread across much of Europe northwards to southern Britain and Ireland. Grows on chalk-rich soils.

139

Further reading

There are many books and publications dealing with the various aspects of European wild flowers. Those listed below will lead you further into this extensive literature.

Clapham, A.R., Tutin, T.G. and Moore, D.M. *Flora of the British Isles* (3rd edition). Cambridge University Press, Cambridge. 1987

Dony, J.G., Jury, S.L. and Perring, F.H. *English Names of Wild Flowers* (2nd edition). The Botanical Society of the British Isles, London. 1986

Grey-Wilson, C. and Blamey, M. *The Alpine Flowers of Britain and Europe*. Collins, London. 1979

Press, R. and Gibbons, R. *Photographic Field Guide to the Wild Flowers of Britain and Europe*. New Holland (Publishers) Ltd, London. 1993

Tutin, T.G. et al (Eds). *Flora Europaea*. 5 volumes. Cambridge University Press, Cambridge. 1964-1981 (Volume 1 revised 1992)

Useful addresses

Botanical Society of the British Isles
c/o Department of Botany, Natural History Museum, Cromwell Road, London SW7 5BD

British Naturalist's Association
48 Russel Way, Higham Ferrers, Northants, NN9 8EJ

English Nature
Northminster House, Peterborough, PE1 1UA

Fauna and Flora Preservation Society
8-12 Camden High Street, London NW1 0JH

Royal Society for Nature Conservation
The Green, Witham Park, Waterside South, Lincoln, LN5 7JR

Wild Flower Society
68 Outwoods Road, Loughborough, Leicestershire, LE11 3LY

Woodland Trust
Autumn Park, Dysart Road, Grantham, Lincs, NG31 6LL

Index

143

144